SHELTON STATE COMMU...
COLLEGE
JUNIOR COLLEGE DIVISION
LIBRARY.

DISCARDED

S0-BIF-592

E
184
.J5
T7

Traditions of the
American Jew

edited by Stanley M.,
Wagner

DATE DUE			
OCT 9 '82			
DEC 11 1993			

TRADITIONS OF THE AMERICAN JEW

TRADITIONS OF
THE AMERICAN JEW

Edited by
STANLEY M. WAGNER

CENTER FOR JUDAIC STUDIES
UNIVERSITY OF DENVER
and
KTAV PUBLISHING HOUSE, INC.
NEW YORK
1977

© COPYRIGHT 1977
STANLEY M. WAGNER

Library of Congress Cataloging in Publication Data
Main entry under title:
Traditions of the American Jew.
    "Delivered originally as part of the J. M. Goodstein
Judaic lecture series."
    Includes bibliographies and index.
    1. Jews in the United States—Addresses, essays, lec-
tures. 2. Judaism—United States—Addresses, essays,
lectures. 3. American literature—Jewish authors—His-
tory and criticism—Addresses, essays, lectures. 4. United
States—Religious life and customs—Addresses, essays,
lectures. I. Wagner, Stanley M.
E184.J5T7   973'.04'924   77-20056
ISBN 0-87068-435-3

MANUFACTURED IN THE UNITED STATES OF AMERICA

This volume is dedicated to
The four most important women
in my life—

Simmy, my *Ayshet Chayil*, help-meet and inspiration;
Frady and Chaya, my beloved daughters and
diadems of *nachas;*

and Mother, who taught me the meaning of
"tradition."

Contents

Introduction

"Tradition" is an important word in the Jewish vocabulary. Its mere mention conjures up thoughts of Tevya's melodious definition in *Fiddler on the Roof*, and of the historical antecedents of the life of a contemporaneous people. More significantly, tradition is the very substance of Jewish civilization—the energizing influence of a folk which has survived the most sinister and overpowering onslaughts, both physical and cultural, to which any nation on the face of the earth has ever been subjected.

Tradition is the thread in the fabric of Jewish existence, or rather the threads, for Jewish tradition is multifold and diverse. Through it the strands of foreign currents, alien ideologies and external influences, have been interwoven—altering, blending with, but never overcoming the unmistakable pattern which identifies Jewish society.

Jewish traditions are not merely values or ideals or orientations to life, transmitted from generation to generation in splendid isolation from the milieu in which they have thrived. While it may be possible to concentrate only on the historical continuity of particular traditions, we would be lacking in perception if we failed to discern the dynamic interaction of those traditions with the peoples and cultures impressing themselves upon the Jewish condition.

This observation is certainly true of Jewish history from the emergence of the Hebrews in biblical times until the age of emancipation, late in the eighteenth century, for until the emancipation the Jews lived a *relatively* insulated existence in corporativistic societies. But it is also true in the post-emancipation world, in which the Jews have lived essentially among the family of nations.

In the post-emancipation world, the mettle of Jewish tradition was tested in one way in Europe and in yet another way in America. On the European continent, the Jews emerged from their ghettos into well-established societies whose centuries-old traditions were firmly ensconced, despite the cultural, technological, and political upheavals of the times. In America, the Jews were among the many immigrant groups for whom rugged individualism and the transformation of traditional life styles were the desiderata.

In this volume we attempt to explore aspects of Jewish tradition as they relate to the American Jewish experience. The articles herein contained are edited lectures presented by renowned and distinguished authorities in their respective fields as part of the J. M. Goodstein Judaic Lecture Series sponsored by the Center for Judaic Studies at the University of Denver.

Each of the chapters focuses upon a particular tradition brought by the Jews to this country, examining its resilience, vitality, and viability in accommodating and adjusting itself to its new environment, as well as the strength of its impact in its new setting. The dynamics of this intriguing dimension of American Jewish life have not been heretofore adequately described, despite the multiplicity of works written on *Americana Judaica*.

The contributions of our authors are always insightful and penetrating; sometimes they startle us. Thus, Trude Weiss-Rosmarin urges that we redefine "culture" as it pertains to the Jew. She insists that the "cultural tradition" of American Jewry does not, as many would believe, manifest itself in participation in the world of aesthetics—music, art, *belles-lettres*. Nor does she agree with Alfred Kazin's assertion that "Jewish culture is what takes place when religion vanishes." Jewish *religious* values are the cornerstones of Jewish culture, protests Dr. Rosmarin, and it is precisely this Jewish cultural tradition, expressed in Jewish perceptions of ethics and morality, of "conscience," which found its way into the democratic striving of the American people. This is the tradition which helped ignite the American passion for unionism, social justice, welfare programs, and philanthropy. The Jewish cultural tradition is manifest in the "Jewish respect for and love of learning," and this explains "the disproportionately large representation of American Jews on the faculties of colleges and universities . . . Their prominence in literature, and in medicine and law." The cultural heritage of the Jew was not only transplanted and preserved in America, it was a catalyst in the transformation of American society.

According to Manheim Shapiro, the ability of the American Jew to contribute so significantly to the growth and development of America, without submerging his own identity, was derived from his European experience, which provided him with a "social tradition" enabling him to adapt, adjust, and acculturate without losing his unique Jewish coloration. The Jew arrived in America with Jewish notions of what it meant to live in a free, egalitarian, just society; he brought with him perceptions of Jewish "peoplehood"; he was familiar with patterns of organizational and institutional life; the family, too, was an important part of his social tradition. These elements in his social makeup also identified the Jew with the ideals of the American creed and vision. The process of "Americanizing for the Jew, however, did not come without its casualties." Shapiro describes the "weakening of two major instrumentalities which had served Jewry in the maintenance of the group and of its mores and standards: the family and the community." For the American Jew, the dangers of assimilation lie in the disintegration of the Jewish family and the rise in the incidence of intermarriage and divorce. Other challenges to the Jewish "social tradition" are found in the dispersal of Jewish neighborhoods, the acceleration of Jewish mobility, the attenuation of Jewish communal controls, and the establishment of a dichotomy of "religious" and "secular" in Jewish community life. Whether the "social tradition" of the American Jew can withstand the battering of these forces remains to be seen.

The religious tradition of the American Jew, declares Abraham J. Karp, cannot be understood except within the context of the antecedent European experiences of "emancipation, enlightenment, and migration" as the counterpart of the American experiences of "freedom, frontier, and immigration." The American Jewish leadership was forced to formulate an indigenously American *religious* response to the threats to Jewish life, especially those of Jewish indifference and willingness to disengage from Jewish communal identification, and the weakening effect of disunity and fragmentization. Attempts at consolidating and amalgamating American Jewry were thwarted, partly because of ideological disparity, partly because the American milieu promoted the proliferation of "sects." The "tripartite religious community" which emerged—Reform, Conservative, and Orthodox synogogue unions and rabbinic seminaries—issued rejoinders to the "melting pot" concept of American life, and then

formulated programs to keep in rhythm with the more contemporaneous American advocacy of "cultural pluralism." Karp maintains that in "the foreseeable future," despite both the centrifugal
and the centripetal forces which act upon Jewish life in America,
"the synagogue will continue to maintain its centrality."

The prominent and successful literary creativity of American
Jewish writers, especially after World War II, is perceived by
David Mirsky to flow from their unique cultural heritage and their
confrontation, as Jews, with the American experience. It is possible
to trace "essential Jewish qualities" manifesting themselves in their
works, "which spring out of and are traceable to Jewish heritage and
tradition." Jewish reverence for the "word" triggered a stylistic
contribution to American literature, asserts Mirsky, reflecting itself
in the establishment of the respectability of rhetoric in American
letters. The Jewish traditional principle of "the sacredness of the
human spirit" impresses itself on, "and, indeed, animates the artistic
creations of many American Jewish writers." But the American
Jewish writer makes his most significant contribution as he comes to
grips with the immigrant experience in America, graphically por-
traying the Jews struggling "with outer reality and inner conflict,"
confronting the "new and alien culture." The alienation and loneliness, the adjustments, the pain and pressures comprised, at one
and the same time, both a Jewish and a universal experience, and
Jewish writers especially were drawn to "explore and probe" its
dynamic. The most successful writers, Mirsky insists, are those who
"directly face up" to themselves as Jews, acknowledging their
"roots within an ancient tradition."

The "political tradition" of the American Jews, according to
Daniel Elazar, emerged out of two struggles: the effort to attain full
and equal rights for themselves, and the reawakening of Jewish
"political interest and concerns"—in essence, the "Jewish pursuit of
the holy commonwealth transposed on the American scene." The
four essential "complexes that have shaped American life," claims
Elazar, correspond to concepts deeply rooted in Jewish life: tradition; agrarianism and its concomitant ethic of self-reliance, family
solidarity, religiosity, and private ownership; federalism, in the
sense of community linkage by covenant under law; and messianism,
an optimistic orientation which propels the people to affirm mankind's potentiality for improvement and to work for its fulfillment.

As a result, "the adaptation of the Jews to American politics was quite rapid," and they zealously, passionately, and continuously exercised their rights as American citizens in the political process, thus, at the same time, accelerating their Americanization. The success of the American Jews in this arena, Elazar atrributes to the openness of American society, the opportunities for economic growth and development which characterize its history, and the confluence of ideologies inherent in the Jewish and the American civilizations. The politics of the contemporary American Jew, however, have assumed a different coloration from the politics of his immediate forebears, which nevertheless may be more related to classical Judaism than its proponents realize.

Our study concludes with David Sidorsky's analysis of the "present condition of the (American) Jewish community and some of the choices that currently confront that community." The interrelationship of the three major Jewish population centers in the world—Russia, Israel, and the United States—will continue to preoccupy American Jewry. Providing us with an historical perspective on this interrelationship, Sidorsky traces the realization of Jewish life in these communities to the major ideological tendencies of nineteenth-century European Jewry—socialism, Zionism, and emancipation. The death of Yiddish culture in America, the destruction of Jewish utopian socialist dreams, and the rise of new forms of American Jewish communal activism relate to the development of Soviet totalitarianism, which "undermined any basis for humanist socialist culture," and generated the tragic plight of Russian Jewry. Although political Zionism was not a major factor in American Jewish life prior to the 1930s, the Holocaust period propelled American Jewry to embrace the Zionist cause, and the State of Israel once established, with an intensity of commitment unparallelled in American Jewish history. The struggle for "emancipation" having been won, the American Jew will nevertheless continue to have emancipation-related issues on his agenda of concern. Sidorsky predicts that problems of church-state relations will challenge, although not polarize, the American Jewish community; that the equation of anti-Zionism and anti-Semitism will perpetuate the need for Jewish "self-defense" efforts and the promotion of intergroup relations; and that the hiatus between those American Jews who are religiously and culturally identified and those who are indifferent and assimilated will continue to grow. How the American Jew will fare in the future, given "the role of human decision and choice" and the unpredictability of events, is uncertain, requiring constant vigilance and concern.

The choices open to the American Jewish community are wide and varied. The freedom to choose, as it pertains to the quality and vitality of Jewish life, can be a blessing or a curse. Whatever the future holds for the American Jew, his "traditions," whether rooted in his history or newly created, will undoubtedly shape his decisions. Self-understanding, hopefully facilitated through this study, will help make those decisions wiser.

This volume is the second in a series published by the Center for Judaic Studies. The first, entitled *Great Confrontations in Jewish History*, attained wide acclaim for its analysis of the encounters between Judaism and paganism, Hellenism, early Christianity, Islam, medieval Christendom, and modern secularism. Our forthcoming work, *Great Schisms in Jewish History*, will explore the inner tensions and ideological conflicts which polarized Jewish life in the past and continue to have their impact upon Jewish life today.

On behalf of the Center, I wish to acknowledge the major contribution of Dorothy and J. M. Goodstein in making possible our first two lecture series and the publications which resulted from them. A debt of gratitude is expressed to Myron (Micky) Miller, Chairman of the University of Denver's Jewish Culture Foundation, which funds the multiple activities of the Center, making it the largest Judaic studies program within a thousand-mile radius of Denver; to Maurice Mitchell, Chancellor of the University, for his perennial support and encouragement. For aid in the publication of this volume I am indebted to Morris Schertz, Director of Libraries at the University, for assisting in the preparation of the Index; and to Bernard Scharfstein of Ktav, for his patience and editorial diligence in bringing this volume to print.

Stanley M. Wagner
Denver, Colorado
August 1977

The Cultural Tradition of the American Jew

TRUDE WEISS-ROSMARIN

JEWISH CULTURE has a continuous and richly documented history of more than three millennia.[1] Although it was created in the proverbial seventy countries of the Jewish dispersion—and in the Land of Israel, of course—this tradition is not delimited by territorial boundaries. The Jewish cultural tradition of the successive principal Jewish centers of Jewish settlement became, almost simultaneously with their creation, the tradition and legacy of all Jews everywhere. The Palestinian and the Babylonian Talmuds,[2] Saadia's and Maimonides' philosophical books, written in Babylonia and Egypt, respectively;[3] Rashi's commentaries, created in Troyes, France;[4] and "Golden Hebrew Poetry" composed in Spain;[5] Joseph Karo's Code, originating in Safed;[6] the hasidic teachings and homilies stemming from Eastern Europe;[7] Mendelssohn's *Jerusalem*, written in Berlin;[8] Graetz's *History*[9] and Hermann Cohen's *Religion of Reason*,[10] exemplifying the best of the *Wissenschaft des Judentums*; Bialik's poems;[11] Ahad Ha-Am's essays;[12] and scores upon scores of other Jewish classics[13] are the cultural tradition of *all* Jews as well as of the American Jew.

My statement that the Jewish cultural tradition is not delimited by territorial boundaries should not be interpreted to imply that time and place did not influence this tradition. They assuredly did, with respect to language, style, and form. However, this influence did not extend to the Jewish core. Like the Jews, who are *one* people and a *unique* people, the Jewish tradition, created in various parts of the world, is yet *one* and also *unique*. To be sure, there are minor differences, for example, between the Ashkenazi and the Sephardi order of prayers[14]—but in all traditional synagogues, everywhere,

1

the principal prayers are the same, and the same biblical and prophetic portions are read on the Sabbaths and the holidays.

The Egyptian loan words in the Pentateuch,[15] the large Greek vocabulary in the Talmud,[16] and the matter-of-fact use of Arabic by the medieval Jewish philosophers, prove that with respect to language the Jewish tradition has not been isolationist, although—and this is of supreme importance—Hebrew has always been regarded as *the* perennial medium of Jewish cultural expression. Even Aramaic and Yiddish, which in the fullest sense of the word are "Jewish languages," have never been accorded the dignity of Hebrew as *lashon hakodesh*—the sacred language. It also must be noted that only those ancient and also more recent books by Jews on Jewish subjects survived which were either written in Hebrew or translated into Hebrew. For example, Philo's works, although of great importance, remained without influence on Jewish thought because, with the eclipse of the Hellenist Jewish center and Philo's ill-luck at not having been translated into Hebrew, his books were inaccessible to Jews, although they were diligently studied by medieval Christian theologians.[17]

Until the age of emancipation and assimilation, ushered in by the French Revolution for the Jews of Western Europe, the influence of the majority cultures on the Jewish culture was limited to linguistic borrowing and "folkways," such as modes of dress and special foods, within the limits of the dietary laws. There was also influence on the *external* accouterments of the Jewish religion, such as synagogue architecture, the styling of Jewish ritual objects, and *niggunim* (musical settings) for prayers. Today, when the so-called Jewish creative arts are assigned a prominent place in the life of the American Jewish community, it should be emphasized that in the Jewish cultural tradition, figurative art figures *only* as craft employed for *hiddur mitzvah*, the "embellishment of the Commandments" with beautiful ritual objects.

Muslim and Christian architecture and art (Islam is, if anything, more iconoclastic than Judaism) influenced synagogue architecture, the styles of Jewish ritual objects, and, also, the illumination and illustration of Hebrew manuscripts and, later, books.[18] But the core of the Jewish tradition remained inviolate and authentically Jewish.

This also is the case with the synagogues in this country, where synagogue architecture, the style of ritual objects, and many of the liturgical melodies are modern-contemporary. However, the Hebrew texts (the English versions of the prayers are *another* matter, of course) are the age- and tradition-hallowed words of the Bible and the prayer book. Irrespective of the modernity of the ark which holds the Torah scrolls, the scrolls are written (written, *not* printed) as commanded by the Law and as they were written throughout the millennia.

"Assimilation" is habitually used in a pejorative sense when associated with "Jewish." But Jews have always assimilated *from* their host cultures. There are two types of assimilation— assimilation *from* the environment, and assimilation *to* the environment. While the latter results in denial of selfhood and thus leads to extinction, assimilation *from* the environment is enriching. For example, linguistic assimilation *from* the host civilization provided the impetus and the material for secondary Jewish languages— Yiddish, Ladino, Judeo-Arabic, Judeo-Persian, and, in antiquity, Aramaic, the predominant language of the Babylonian Talmud and, also, of some parts of the Bible.

However, the varieties of local Jewish customs, style, and secondary Jewish vernaculars—and even the vast typological differences between Jews of different continents and countries, to wit, the contrast between the swarthy Yemenites and the fair-skinned Western Jews—did not impinge upon the Jewish cultural tradition. Indeed, Yemenites pronounce Hebrew gutturally, as it must be pronounced if one is to differentiate correctly between *alef* and *ayin* and between *het* and *kaf*; American Jews impart to the Hebrew vowels an American tonality, to wit, their pronunciation of *shalom*—their mark of identification in Israel. But these regional differences of pronunciation—and there are others which are more important—are insignificant compared to the unitary and enduring core of the Jewish tradition, which is the same—and this must be emphasized—again and again—for all Jews wherever they may be. It is because of this shared core of tradition and history that Jews in their many habitations have always regarded themselves—and still regard themselves—as "one people."

The recognition of ethnic-cultural *peoplehood* as distinguished from political *nationhood* is a very recent American "discovery." Like most new insights, it must wage an uphill struggle—in this instance, against the deep-seated suspicion that "ethnics" have divided loyalties. Jews, because of a history plagued with political adversity and homelessness, "discovered" *peoplehood*, as distinguished from *nationhood*, some twenty-seven centuries ago, after the destruction of the First Temple (586 B.C.E.), when Jeremiah admonished those who were carried away as captives to Babylonia: "Build houses and live in them, plant gardens and eat their produce . . . seek the welfare of the city where I have sent you into exile, and pray to the Lord on its behalf, for in its welfare you will find your welfare" (Jer. 29:6 f.). However, Jeremiah also sustained the exiles' *peoplehood* identity and hopes by the Divine promise of restoration on the ancestral soil. The majority of the children and grandchildren of the exiled Judeans chose to remain in Babylonia after the Persian conquest and Xerxes' "Declaration," which made possible the Return to Judea under Zerubbabel, Ezra, and Nehemiah. They stayed on in their exile and built houses, planted gardens, and raised families. They prospered and increased in numbers, and they prayed for the welfare of their cities and their adopted country. But they also remained, religiously and culturally, "a people dwelling apart." The full extent of their cultural-religious separateness is evident from the flowering of their Talmud academies, whose fruits were harvested in the Babylonian Talmud.

If one is to do justice to the cultural tradition of American Jews, one must beware of the temptation of assigning too large a role to the *shtetl* memories, especially its nostalgic celebration in the popular culture of the stage, screen, and "hasidic happenings." Indeed, the East European Jews of the little towns were faithful guardians of the Jewish cultural tradition—guardians and interpreters—but not innovative creators. Moreover, notwithstanding the current enthusiasm for (usually inauthentic) hasidic celebrations and the idealization of *shtetl* life, one would be unfair—to say nothing of the offense to scholarship—if one were to trace the cultural tradition of the American Jews to "the old home" in Europe of the last two decades of the nineteenth century and the pre-World War I years.[19]

So as to do justice to the essence of the Jewish cultural tradition—a tradition shared by all Jews everywhere—one must focus on the distinctive values which brought this tradition into being, entrenched it, and made possible its creative unfolding.

There is, first and foremost, the Jewish tradition of assigning to education the top rung in its scale of values. Knowledge of the Torah outranks even piety because "the ignoramus [am ha-aretz] cannot be pious."[20] There are good reasons why Jews "compose about half of the American intellectual elite," although they constitute less than 3 percent of the American population.[21] Intellectual élitism is a Jewish religious imperative. It is implicit in the idea of Jewish chosenness, understood and interpreted throughout the ages as the *obligation* to become worthy of the Covenant—worthy by the insight that accrues from knowledge and leads one to do right and shun wrong. The disproportionately large representation of American Jews on the faculties of colleges and universities, especially the so-called Ivy League colleges,[22] their prominence in literature, in pure and applied research, and in medicine and law—an over-representation, statistically, is the modern expression of the traditional Jewish respect for and love of learning.

No sooner were the ghetto restrictions in Europe rescinded than Jewish youths flocked to the universities in numbers vastly disproportionate to the Jewish representation in the general population. And before long the "outsider," as the Jew was seen, became the "insider" who to a very large extent set the style and quality of the general culture, notably during the Weimar Republic. Peter Gay and others have documented how the preeminence of Jews in the "Weimar Culture" contributed to intensifying Nazi anti-Semitism.[23] There is no doubt that Jewish intellectual preeminence and over-representation are resented. On the Jewish side, there have been various unsuccessful attempts—by organizations and individual philanthropists—to effect a more "normal" Jewish occupational pattern.[24] However, even in the Israeli kibbutzim, where manual labor is a status value, the children of the founders stream to the universities.

The respect and desire for learning has been so diligently and persistently *nurtured* by Jews that, as a consequence of this nurturing, it has become the most distinctive characteristic of Jewishness. However, literacy was widespread, if not universal, in ancient Israel, centuries before Joshua ben Gamala decreed compulsory education for boys, starting at the age of six, about two thousand years ago.[25] (Girls were excluded from schooling—this was a universal evil.) Jews were first in legislating for compulsory universal education.[26] As for literacy in Bible times, the tradition that Gideon could demand of a boy he chanced to capture at Succoth to write down for him the names of the seventy-seven princes and elders of Succoth (Judg. 8:14) is strong evidence that reading and writing were not limited to a special class or caste in ancient Israel.

In the Jewish tradition, learning is commanded, not merely recommended. It is a *mitzvah* to be observed all the days of one's life.[27] Adult education, in this country and elsewhere as well, is a recent response to the problem and mixed blessing of leisure afforded by the thirty-five hour or thirty-hour work week and especially by retirement at an age when most senior citizens still have five or more years of good health and too many empty hours to look forward to. Judaism considers lifelong learning as important as the schooling of children and youths. The Pentateuch commands continuing education for the duration of life. One is to speak about the words of the Torah "when you lie down and when you get up, when you are at home and when you are pursuing your way."

Recently, Dr. Ernest L. Boyer, chancellor of the State University of New York, deplored that higher education is "focused almost exclusively on one age group, students who have come in just four sizes: 18, 19, 20 and 21." Dr. Boyer demanded provision for "higher education for all, through old age . . . as a resource for everyone from 18 to 85 and beyond." So as to make it possible for adults "to weave periods of formal and informal study into the working years," he suggested that the sabbatical should not be limited "to a tiny minority of the academic élite." All Americans should have the opportunity to take sabbatical leaves so as "to enrich themselves intellectually and refine their working skills." He proposed that "the freedom to learn, whatever the age, whatever the stage in life," should be added as the Fifth Freedom to the Four Freedoms proclaimed by Franklin D. Roosevelt.[28]

Boyer's program of "higher education for all, through old age," is not utopian. It has been the norm of education in the traditional Jewish community for more than two thousand years. Moreover, in the Jewish society, "the freedom to learn" was implemented and reinforced with the categorical imperative to study Torah—a legal obligation.

Maimonides' Code summarizes the laws pertaining to the duty of Torah study as follows: "Every Jew is obligated to study Torah, whether he be rich or poor, healthy or sick, in the bloom of youth or aged and weak. Even the pauper who is supported by charity or goes begging from door to door, and he who has a wife and children to support must set aside fixed periods by day and night for the study of the Torah."[29]

More than a thousand years before Maimonides (1135–1204), Hillel the Elder addressed himself to the problem of making time for study. As Hillel saw it, waiting for leisure is procrastination and hoping for what may never materialize. This is why one must not say: "I shall study when I have leisure to do so." Hillel asked: "What if you never have leisure?"[30] In the same spirit, Maimonides warned: "If you say, I shall study after having put aside some money and provided for my necessities . . . you will never be worthy of the crown of the Torah."[31] Study of the Torah must be integrated into the daily routine. How this was accomplished is documented by the last wills of medieval Jews who bequeathed to their children rules and guidance for Torah study, such as the following:

> There are two appropriate times for regular daily study of Torah: (1) In the morning before breakfast, immediately after morning prayers. Nothing must be permitted to interfere with this habit. . . . At any rate, never leave home, not even on pressing business, before studying a passage. . . . (2) At night, immediately after supper, and again before retiring. It is advisable to study early in the evening, before supper, either the whole or the better part of the set portion, for eating makes one sleepy and then one cannot study effectively.[32]

There were ample and variegated communal facilities of adult education. Even tiny Jewish communities had a *Hevra Tehillim*

(Psalms study group), a *Hevra Mishnayot* (Mishna study group), and a *Hevra Shas* (Talmud study group) meeting daily or several times a week.[33]

As for the "sabbaticals" of Dr. Boyer's "higher education for all" program, they were part and parcel of Jewish life during the talmudic and gaonic periods in Babylonia (ca. 200–1100), when for one month at the end of the winter (Adar) and one month at the end of the summer (Elul), thousands of Jews from all walks of life journeyed to the Talmud Academies for *Yarhei Kallah*—the Kallah Months of study (scholars are divided on whether *kallah*, in this context, means "bride," i.e., the Torah, or "completion," i.e., the end of a semester of study).

The various talmudic descriptions of *Yarhei Kallah*[34] provide the profile of a serious and intensive "continuing education" project for students at all levels of competence, including conferences for leading scholars. There were public lectures by the heads of the Yeshivot, implemented by study groups and individual study, all concentrated on one theme—"the *Kallah* tractate" for which everybody had prepared in the interval since the previous *Kallah*. "Open admission" was (as it still is) the policy of the Yeshivot and also of the *Yarhei Kallah* assemblies—there were no proficiency tests and no final examinations: The discipline in this completely voluntary system of education was a discipline of motivation. Those who shared in *Yarhei Kallah* studies differed in knowledge and also in intelligence. But they managed, as Yeshiva students do today, to study on their respective levels, and even above, thanks to the stimulation of the general atmosphere of high expectations and, more important, by being paired for preparation and follow-up study with a more advanced fellow-student in a *Havrutha* (companionate study).

The Babylonian Jews amazed and also annoyed their non-Jewish neighbors when they closed down their businesses and suspended their activities for two months of *Kallah* studies. "Vacationing" for study involved great economic hardships. The Talmud records that, at one time, some twelve thousand *Kallah* participants lacked the funds to pay their taxes to the royal treasury.[35] Like the weekly Sabbath of rest and the periodic rest periods of the holidays, the

Kallah months of study were a unique Jewish innovation at a time when the social conscience of the great nations of antiquity was insensitive to the human needs of the laboring masses of slaves, especially the need for rest and education. Judaism posits that freedom is inextricably bound to knowledge. Just as the ignorant cannot be pious, so they cannot be free and make knowledgeable choices. By an ingenious play on the Hebrew word *haroot* ("incised" in the passage "The tablets were God's work, and the writing was God's writing, *incised* upon the tablets," Exod. 32:16), which by changing the vowels can be read *heiroot* ("freedom"), the Rabbis established an organic bond between knowledge and freedom.

Because of its emphasis on the study of Torah—Torah signifying "this Torah which Moses set before the Children of Israel" and its many commentaries and expositions—the Jewish culture is a culture of *the word*. It is literature, books—and books of a special kind, as we shall see.

In essence, the word is an abstraction and conceptualization of the tangibly sensate. The Jewish aversion—it is *aversion* and not merely rejection—to the concretization of God permeates the Hebrew Bible and is most articulately expressed in *I am that I am* (Exod. 3:14), God's self-definition in reply to Moses' question concerning the Divine name. *I am that I am* divests God of all that is physical, defining him as *Being As Such*—Absolute Being—beyond description, except in metaphor, and beyond representation in a medium of art. The demythologization[36] of God (and nature, as well) in ancient Israel is the reason—and there is no cause for regret!—that the ancient Hebrew did not leave a legacy of art comparable to that of the great and small nations of the ancient Near and Middle East. The commandment "you shall not make for yourself a graven image, nor any manner of likeness, of anything that is in heaven above, or that is on the earth, or that is in the water" (Exod. 20:3) was aimed at uprooting idol worship. *But* the rationale of the prohibition of idol worship is that it precludes the achievement of the unique human faculty, conceptualization.

Israel's road to the achievement of conceptualization was long and arduous—and there were constant backslidings. Time and again the children of Israel yearned and clamored for "a god who shall go before us," a god who can be seen and touched, a god who is *real* to the senses. It is hard to believe in a god who proclaims: "Man shall not see me and live." It is much more reassuring to lay one's sacrifices and one's prayers before a god who *can* be seen and touched.

Almost up to our own time, art was either religious art or closely identified with religion. Most kings of the realms of the ancient Middle East were revered as gods and traced their descent from the gods. Their statues were not "portraits" in the modern sense but cult objects. Greece and Rome, at the height of their cultural efflorescence, had advanced beyond the primitive beliefs which were at the roots of Sumerian, Babylonian, and Assyrian temple art and the Egyptian cult of the dead, which produced the pyramids and exquisite art. But Greek and Roman art, too, were cult-centered, even after Greek and Roman philosophy had shaken the belief in the gods.

European art, throughout the Middle Ages and well into the modern era, was principally religious art. The Catholic Church was the great patron of the arts so as to instruct the Catholic populations, among whom literacy was the exception rather than the rule. Compulsory general education has a history of little more than a century in Europe and in this country. In the Middle Ages and far into the modern era, the knowledge of reading and writing was limited to the clergy and the small group of those with means and a desire to exercise their minds. The Church needed canvas and statue to teach illiterates the fundamentals of the Christian faith.

Pictorial art is now being assigned a great importance in American Jewish culture, analogous to its role in the American culture. However, the adulation of art is alien to the Jewish tradition, and for valid reasons, principally because art is a turning away from life. *Art is life arrested;* it is life deprived of breath and movement. The work of art is the fixation of only one moment.[37]

Among the key words of Judaism, *sefer ha-hayyim*—the Book of Life—ranks prominently. The Book of Life, in Jewish interpretation, is life in its totality, and to read this "book" means involvement and personal identification with life—the readiness and willingness to *act*, so as to bring one's own contribution to bear upon life.

The artist creates "from" life but not "in" and "with" life. He paints a portrait which will live long after the one who sits for it has been reduced to dust—but the portrait and the statue only simulate life.

The work of art is the re-creation of nature by the artist. It is a reading of the Book of Life from which life has been drained.

Art is man's way of competing with God—his only way. Jews, too, have aspired and dreamed of creating in the manner of God. The *Golem* saga attests this quest and the despair which comes with the realization that all that man can create, even in alliance with the Name of God, is a *Golem*, a reason-bereft and goodness-deprived automaton.[38]

Authentic Jewish creativity does not aim at *re*-creating life and creating *from* life, in the manner of the artist. Jewish creativity aims at reshaping life by infusing life in its totality with meaning and purpose. This dedication to *life* means that one dare not assume the stance of an "observer" from the outside, in the manner of the artist and writer.

"Compassion," this much overworked cliché of literary criticism, is for the Jew not something to be spent and exhausted in *description*, but a call to *action*. It is not enough to "describe" suffering and make of it a work of art. Compassion, as Judaism defines it, means to alleviate the suffering of the sufferer by action, even if it is only listening to his woes and extending the hand as a sign of "suffering with," i.e., compassion. Compassion, as Judaism sees it, must not be arrested on the level of art. Compassion requires action on behalf of the sufferer.

As a result of what may be termed a "social action" orientation, the tradition of Jewish literature shows little inclination to *belles-lettres*. The description of literature as fiction, drama, and poetry—a definition which is also applied to American Jewish literature—is not in the spirit of the Jewish tradition. The "Great Jewish Books" are not novels, dramas, and nondidactic verse. They are books that are frankly didactic. They teach how to live not "the good life" but the life that *is* good in deeds. They are books of law and of ethics, because law is the basis and guarantee of ethics, even as ethics is the flowering of the good which law is meant to bring about and guard.

In the introduction to his "Lifetime Reading Plan," Clifton

Fadiman wrote: "Remember that these books [the world's great classics] are not only to be read. They are to be reread. They are not like a current novel. They are inexhaustible. Plato read at twenty-five is one man, Plato read at forty-five still another."

The great Jewish books, too, "are not like a current novel." The great Jewish books are inexhaustible and must be reread and reread. And because great books are not to be read "like a current novel"—or a novel that was current yesterday—the cultural tradition of the American Jew is not rooted in Mendele, Peretz, Sholom Aleichem, and their less well known contemporaries who created a tradition of Yiddish fiction. Nor is this tradition to be associated with Abraham Cahan's early novel *The Rise of David Levinsky* or, today, with Isaac Bashevis Singer, Bellow, Malamud, and the Roths—Henry and Philip. The *Jewish* importance bestowed upon them by those who would define Jewish culture in the generally accepted sense is, in fact, nonexistent. To qualify as *Jewish* books, books must *teach values*, not entertain. They must teach ethics and morals, also today when such standards are "old-fashioned," and vulgarity and pornography are "trendy" and are being celebrated as "culture." In my scale of values, the contemporary writer of American Jewish fiction who qualifies as a *teacher*—and a Jewish writer *must* teach or he cannot lay claim to being a *Jewish* writer—is Chaim Potok.

Potok is not taken "seriously" by the literary critics who acclaim Bellow and Philip Roth. Potok's novels are bare of four-letter words and of explicit descriptions of sex. Still, his books, including his latest novel, *In the Beginning*, are best-sellers in the hardcover editions and sell millions of copies as paperbacks. Potok is a gifted storyteller but—and this is more important—what matters in the context of Jewish tradition is that his novels *teach* Jewish values: dedication to Torah study and observance, loyalty to family and friends, sacrificial readiness for ideas and ideals. They also *teach* how the Talmud and the Bible are studied by tradition-bound scholars and by modern, tradition-respecting scholars. Potok's books have made an invaluable contribution to Jewish literacy and to interpreting Judaism to non-Jews. I don't know whether they are great books for the ages, but they are contemporary American expressions of the Jewish cultural tradition of the ages.

The first major Jewish celebration of the Bicentennial was a Conference on Jewish Cultural Arts under the auspices of the National Jewish Welfare Board. One of its events was a symposium on "Literature and Writers" for the purpose of defining Jewish culture. Alfred Kazin, the noted literary critic, asserted that "Jewish culture is what takes place when religion vanishes." Dr. Kazin, Distinguished Professor of English at Hunter College, and Dr. Richard Gilman, Professor of Drama at Yale University, agreed that "space is cleared for creativity, in literature as well as plastic arts, when orthodoxy is defeated or put aside—as though concentration on the Creation inhibits man's creations."[39]

The authentic Jewish cultural tradition and its values did not fare well at that symposium, which exemplified the emphasis on the "cultural arts"—theater, dance, music, painting, sculpture, and *belles-lettres* in post–World War II America and in the American Jewish community.

New York is said to have displaced Paris as the world capital of art, what with some hundreds of art galleries prospering in Manhattan, which also has three museums of modern art in addition to the Metropolitan and the Frick. The theater, the ballet, and music are flourishing all over the United States, and not only in New York. And as modern Jews tend to be in the vanguard and part of the avant-garde of general culture, the American Jewish scene is astir with the "creative arts."

But *are* the creative arts *culture* as Judaism defines culture? Do they enhance the ethical-moral quality of life? The answer is *NO*. We, in our own time, have seen the Germans, a nation steeped and excelling in the creative arts, commit barbarous mass murder on an unprecedented scale and with unimaginable beastliness. Hitler, a failed painter, was an ardent collector and lover of art, who had turned his Berchtesgaden castle into a veritable museum. Mengele, who was in charge of the Auschwitz selections—the physically fit for hard labor, the children, the aged, and the weak for the gas chambers and the ovens—was an avid concert-goer and a collector of classical music records. While consigning masses of Jews, and also non-Jewish "undesirables" as defined by the Nazi code, to the Final Solution, he whistled and hummed Mozart and Beethoven.

That the creative arts are not conducive to the development of conscience and ethics is a fact of history.[40] In antiquity, the efflorescence of art—in ancient Babylonia and Egypt, and, later, in Greece and Rome—did not inhibit brutality toward slaves, women, and children, the abuse of those who did not belong to the ruling class. Closer to our own time, in the late fifteenth and the sixteenth century, the Medicis, thanks to their generous support of artists and poets, made Florence unsurpassed in artistic achievements. But the Medicis also excelled in brutality and corruption.

Focusing upon our own American society and the Jewish community, one notes that the post–World War II efflorescence of the creative arts coincides with a monumental rise in juvenile delinquency and crime, drug addiction, alcoholism, the breakdown of the family, and the flaunting of the values which are the basis of the Jewish culture and by which the founders of this country lived. In New York's Lincoln Center and nearby Carnegie Hall, more than ten thousand persons assemble on an average evening for opera, concerts, the ballet, and theater. But close to this great center of the creative arts, tens of thousands of old and forsaken men and women are hungry and cold—and at the mercy of muggers and murderers.

In New York there are more than a quarter of a million old and poor Jews, many of them housebound invalids and tragically lonely. They have been left behind in what were once upon a time middle-class neighborhoods. Their children have moved to the suburbs, where cultural arts activities flourish. There is no time for the "old folks," because the *art of Jewish living* is not in vogue. This art, as Hermann Cohen defined it, is achieving *correlation*[41]—Buber called it *dialogue*[42]—with our fellow-humans, and first of all with our own kith and kin.

The creative arts, we are told, have therapeutic value—filling the empty hours of people who find relief-and-release in painting, sculpting, writing, and play-acting as *amateurs*. It is estimated that there are about twenty million "Sunday painters" in this country, and several million women are said to have a novel-in-progress next to their file of recipes. But judging by the flood of self-help and do-your-own-analysis books, and the huge consumption of tran-quilizers, it would seem that the "culture consumers" and the amateur practitioners of the creative arts are not finding release and relief.

Perhaps if these people were to use their leisure hours and empty days in keeping with the pattern of the Jewish cultural tradition, their boredom, restlessness, and sense of unfulfillment would give way to *simchah shel mitzvah*—the joy which comes with the fulfillment of the commandments of *personal* social service: visiting the sick, comforting mourners, honoring parents and *all* aged people by not shunting them into "senior citizens" clubs and "adult communities," but keeping them in our midst as valued and respected members of the community.

Bioethics is a new word, so new that as yet it is not listed in the dictionaries. Bioethics is an interdisciplinary academic enterprise for the ethical study of the religious implications of new medical procedures and, also, new definitions of life and death. Jewish tradition and law have much to say on bioethics. However, in the context of my theme, I shall forgo citing Jewish law on such medical problems of bioethics as brain death, euthanasia, abortion, experimenting with fetal tissue, and resorting to extraordinary means for supporting the life processes of a patient in an irreversible coma.[43] In the context of tracing the tradition inherited by the American Jew, it is all-important to state that Jewish ethics is bioethics in the literal sense. It is *torat hayyim*—teaching-and-law unequivocally committed to protect and nurture life in all its manifestations and, especially, human life as the "image of God."

Jewish bioethics posits that man is the supreme value—*every* person, because *every* person reflects the image of God, as it were. Modern and contemporary thinkers have warned against the depersonalization of Western societies as a consequence of the overvaluation of the machine. They have decried the worship of technology as idolatry as destructive of human and humane values as were the ancient idolatries that worshipped nature and demanded human sacrifices to be offered up on idolatrous altars.

James H. Breasted, the eminent Egyptologist, held that Western civilization, although born in Egypt, was transmitted to the Western world by the Jews. In his *The Dawn of Conscience*, Breasted marveled at "the extraordinary fact that this great [Egyptian] moral legacy should have descended to Western civilization from a politically insignificant people," i.e., the Jews. Breasted's pan-Egyptian orientation, which was uncritically accepted by Freud in his *Moses and Monotheism*, was the notion of Egyptologists exclusively.[44]

The ancient Hebrews, as we have seen, did not bequeath to posterity splendiferous palaces and art. Their legacy is *conscience*. Conscience "dawned" among the ancient Hebrews, and it reached its zenith in the Pentateuchal legislation. Conscience, as defined by Judaism, means being conscious of the fact that we *are* accountable for our fellowmen when asked: "Where is your brother?" (Gen. 4:9). In the context of Jewish bioethics, understood as *torat hayyim*, "Where is your brother?" means: What is your fellowmen's situation? What are their needs? Are they hungry? Is their situation such that it degrades their human dignity?

Conscience, as Judaism interprets it, means concern about our fellowmen—concern suffused with respect. It is this respect for man as a reflection of the Divine image which is the motivation for "proclaiming liberty throughout all the land" (Lev. 25:10). The four freedoms of the Roosevelt-Churchill Atlantic Charter—freedom of speech, freedom of religion, freedom from fear, and freedom from want—were first proclaimed and secured by Jewish law and ethics.[45] Moreover, these freedoms were not rhetoric but norms of life, as is attested by the Hebrew Bible. When American patriots proclaimed that "rebellion against tyrants is obedience to God," they identified with the Hebrews, who were enslaved by and rebelled against Pharaoh, as they were enslaved by and rebelled against the British. Rebels for a cause have always drawn inspiration from the Exodus as well as from the Hebrew Prophets, who opposed the high and mighty of their day.

The Hebrew tradition of protest for conscience's sake was well developed centuries before the "writing Prophets," to wit, Nathan's condemnation of King David for taking the wife of Uriah and conspiring in the "accidental death" of her husband. Where in the ancient world would a man have dared to chastise the king for taking a woman he desired? And where in the ancient world would a king have humbly acknowledged that this was sin? Few of today's clergymen would dare to upbraid a member of their congregation in the manner Nathan tongue-lashed David.

The ancient Hebrews even spoke and protested against, and *argued* with, God. When Sodom and Gomorrah were to be destroyed, Abraham demanded of God: "Will You really sweep away the good along with the evil?" (Gen. 18:24 ff.). And when God announced that He would annihilate the Israelites because of Korah's sin, Moses and Aaron challenged Him: "When one man sin, will You be angry with the whole congregation?" (Num. 16:21)— and God reconsidered and punished only the sinners.

The Jewish labor leaders in this country who pioneered unionism were in the mainstream of the Hebrew prophetic tradition. They denounced and fought against the exploitation of the workers, as Amos did some twenty-seven centuries ago.

Social Security, too, has roots in the Jewish tradition. Our Social Security system is predicated on the Jewish conviction that provision for the "underprivileged" must not be left to the vagaries of "love" ("charity" is derived from the Latin *caritas*—"love"), but must be legislated. The Hebrew word for "charity" is *tzedakah*—meaning *justice*. According to Maimonides, "gifts to the poor are not donations but debts one owes as of law."

Organized Jewish charity—the oldest social service system of which we know—has a history of over two thousand years, predating the destruction of the Second Temple (70 C.E.). Already in those remote days, Jewish communities raised and administered relief funds—one for major and regular relief, and one for emergency, short-term assistance. All members of the Jewish community were "taxed" for these funds, although the amount was left to their conscience. However, if those in charge of collecting the tax money had reason to suspect that an individual gave less than the tithe of 10 percent, legal proceedings could be instituted for the collection of the *lawful* amount. Until emancipation, Jewish self-government was the norm, and the rabbinical courts could and did attach the property of delinquent tithe payers.[46]

With respect to freedom of religion, the architects of Judaism anticipated by more than two millennia the Constitution of the United States. Judaism grants freedom of religion provided it does not injure public welfare. For example, adult members of certain Christian sects are free to reject medical treatment and blood transfusions, but in the case of minors, physicians can obtain court orders permitting them to operate or give blood transfusions to children over the "religious protest" of the parents. In Judaism, as in American law, the presumption is that "freedom of religion" does not mean freedom for injurious actions in the name of God.

The Bill of Rights limits the power of government lest it interfere with "life, liberty and the pursuit of happiness." Everywhere, almost until our own time, and in the Communist countries today, the masses stood in fear of the high and the mighty who wielded absolute power and were *above* the law. Not so in ancient Israel, however. There was a single standard for ruler and subject. How this single standard was operative may be seen from the narrative about Naboth's vineyard (I Kings 21). It is immaterial whether the event described is "historical" or "symbolic." What matters is that it is taken for granted that the king of Israel *cannot* appropriate the possession of one of his subjects against the man's will, even if he is fully indemnified. Characteristically, Ahab's wife, Jezebel, a daughter of the king of Tyre, thought her husband was compromising his royal honor by accepting Naboth's answer: "I shall not give my vineyard to you." In the authoritarian-absolutist manner of Israel's neighbors, she had Naboth murdered and his vineyard confiscated.

The Bill of Rights provides that every American has access to the courts so as to sue for his rights. The Bill of Rights stands for the constitutional right of peaceful assembly, and guarantees freedom of speech and freedom of religion.

The American idea is the sum total of the great liberties based on the belief in the unique and unlimited worth and dignity of every person because man *is* created in the image of God. The commitment to this belief and all that flows from it made Israel a unique people. It made the Bible the singular book which has nurtured Western civilization and guided and inspired the Founding Fathers of this country. The great liberties proclaimed in 1776 derived from the impact of the Book which was the constant companion and guide of the authors of our Constitution. The Book they revered as holy provided the paradigm of ancient Israel with its government of the people, by the people, and for the people, under God and in freedom.

NOTES

1. The Jewish culture is a religious culture, and thus its history is the history of Judaism. An up-to-date, popular, and comprehensive overview of the Jewish culture is Daniel J. Silver and Bernard Martin, *A History of Judaism*, 2 vols. (New York, 1974).

2. The Babylonian Talmud is available in the standard English translation in I. Epstein, trans., *The Babylonian Talmud*, 36 vols. (London, 1935–48). There are several good talmudic anthologies, notably C. G. Montefiore and H. Loewe, *A Rabbinic Anthology* (London, 1938), and A. Cohen, *Everyman's Talmud* (London, 1932). Both are available in paperback reprints. For an introduction and survey of the Talmud, see Adin Steinsalz, *The Essential Talmud* (New York, 1976).

3. Saadia Gaon, *The Book of Belief and Doctrines*, trans. Samuel Rosenblatt (New Haven, 1948); Moses Maimonides, *The Guide of the Perplexed*, trans. Shlomo Pines with an introductory essay by Leo Strauss (Chicago, 1963).

4. Thus far, only Rashi's commentary on the Pentateuch has been translated into English: M. Rosenbaum and A. M. Silbermann, trans., *Pentateuch With Targum Onkelos, Haphtaroth and Rashi's Commentary* (London, 1929–34).

5. Israel Zangwill, trans., *Selected Religious Poems of Solomon Ibn Gabirol* (Philadelphia, 1974), paperback; Nina Salaman, trans., *Selected Poems of Jehudah Halevi* (Philadelphia, 1974), paperback; Solomon Solis-Cohen, trans., *Selected Poems of Moses Ibn Ezra* (Philadelphia, 1945); Leon J. Weinberger, trans., *Jewish Prince in Moslem Spain: Selected Poems of Samuel Ibn Nagrella* University of Alabama, 1973).

6. Karo's *Shulchan Arukh* [Set Table] has been condensed and translated. The condensation by Solomon Ganzfried, known as *Kitzur Shulchan Arukh*, was translated into English by Hyman E. Goldin. It is available in several editions, besides the New York edition (Hebrew Publishing Co.) of 1927.

7. There are a number of hasidic anthologies and collections of stories. They all draw on Martin Buber's *Tales of the Hasidim*, trans. Olga Marx, 2 vols. (New York, 1947).

8. Moses Mendelssohn, *Jerusalem: A Treatise on Ecclesiastical Authority and Judaism*, trans. M. Samuels, 2 vols. (London, 1838); Alfred Jospe, trans. and ed., *Jerusalem and Other Jewish Writings by Moses Mendelssohn* (New York, 1969).

9. H. Graetz, *History of the Jews*, 6 vols. (New York, 1927).

10. Hermann Cohen, *Religion of Reason Out Of The Sources of Judaism*, trans. Simon Kaplan (New York, 1972).

11. Hayyim Nahman Bialik, *Complete Poetic Works*, trans. Israel Efros (New York, 1948); Maurice Samuel, trans., *Selected Poems by Chaim Nachman Bialik* (New York, 1972).

12. Ahad Ha-Am, *Essays, Letters, Memoirs*, trans. Leon Simon (Oxford, 1946).

13. Meyer Waxman, *A History of Jewish Literature from the Close of the Bible to Our Own Day*, 4 vols. (New York, 1930–41); Israel Zinberg, *A History of Jewish Literature*, trans. from the Yiddish by Bernard Martin, 11 vols. to date, vol. 12 is scheduled for publication in 1978 (Cleveland and New York, 1972–); Reuben Wallenrod, *The Literature of Modern Israel* (New York and London, 1956); Simon Halkin, *Modern Hebrew Literature* (New York, 1950); Charles Madison, *Yiddish Literature from Mendele and Sholom Aleichem to Isaac Bashevis Singer* (New York, 1968).

14. H. J. Zimmels, *Ashkenazim and Sephardim* (London, 1958), pp. 324 ff.;

Raphael Posner, Uri Kaploun, and Shalom Dohen, eds., *Jewish Liturgy: Prayer and Synagogue Service Through the Ages* (New York and Paris, 1975).

15. A. S. Yahuda, *The Accuracy of the Bible* (New York, 1935).
16. Saul Lieberman, *Greek in Jewish Palestine* (New York, 1942).
17. H. A. Wolfson, *Philo*, 2 vols. (Cambridge, Mass., 1947), 1:289 ff., 456 ff., 2:428 ff.
18. Joseph Gutmann, ed., *Beauty in Holiness: Studies in Jewish Customs and Ceremonial Art* (New York, 1970); Heinrich Strauss, *Die Kunst der Juden im Wandel der Zeit und Umwelt* (Tuebingen, 1972).
19. Irving Howe, *The World of Our Fathers* (New York, 1976), is typical of giving the *shtetl* and its tradition more than their due while disregarding the long Hebraic tradition which was the ground from which the Yiddish culture of the *shtetl* grew.
20. Mishnah, Avot II, 45.
21. Charles Kadushin, *The American Intellectual Elite* (Boston, 1974), pp. 23 ff.
22. Everett Carll Ladd, Jr., and Seymour Martin Lipset, *The Divided Academy* (New York, 1975), pp. 149–67.
23. Peter Gay, "Weimar Culture: The Outsider as Insider," in *The Intellectual Migration*, ed. Donald Fleming and Bernard Bailyn (Cambridge, Mass., 1969), pp. 11–94; Walter Laqueur, *Weimar* (New York, 1974).
24. Mark Wischnitzer, *History of Jewish Crafts and Guilds* (New York, 1965).
25. Babylonian Talmud, *Megilah* 32a.
26. Study is compulsory for all male children and youths as well as for adult males, in accordance with the biblical commandment, Deut. 7:6.
27. Adult education in Judaism from biblical times to the twentieth century is the theme of Israel M. Goldman, *Lifelong Learning Among Jews* (New York; 1975).
28. *New York Times*, 8 April 1974, "Op-Ed" page.
29. Maimonides, *Hilkhot Talmud Torah* I, 8, quoted by Goldman, op. cit., p. 136.
30. Mishnah, Avot II, 5.
31. Ibid. I, 15.
32. Maimonides, op. cit., III, 7, quoted by Goldman, p. 139.
33. Goldman, pp. 74 ff.; Jacob Lauterbach, "The Name of the Rabbinical Schools and Assemblies in Babylonia," *Hebrew Union College Jubilee Volume* (Cincinnati, 1925), pp. 211–22.
34. Goldman, chaps. 10, 11.
35. Babylonian Talmud, *Baba Metzi'ah* 86a.
36. Ernst Cassirer, *The Philosophy of Symbolic Forms* (New Haven, 1955), vol. 2, pp. 49, 55, 252; Trude Weiss-Rosmarin, "Demythologizing the Hebrew Bible," *Conservative Judaism 23* (1969): 51–59.
37. Trude Weiss-Rosmarin, "The Jewish Meaning of Art," in *Annals of the Jewish Academy of Arts and Sciences* (New York, 1974), pp. 135–54.
38. Norbert Wiener, *God and Golem, Inc.* (Cambridge, Mass., 1964).
39. *New York Times*, 13 January 1976, p. 42.
40. George Steiner, *In Bluebeard's Castle: Some Notes Towards the Redefinition of Culture* (New Haven, 1971).
41. Hermann Cohen, *Religion of Reason*, chap. 8.
42. Martin Buber, *I and Thou*, available in several paperback editions.
43. Immanuel Jakobovits, *Jewish Medical Ethics* (New York, 1959). For more recent articles, see indices of *Jewish Tradition*.

44. Freud's hypothesis of the *Egyptian* Moses was rejected even by Freudians. Gregory Zilboorg, *Freud and Religion* (Westminster, Md., 1958), pp. 34–45; Ernest Jones, *The Life and Work of Sigmund Freud* (New York, 1953–57), vol. 3, pp. 370 ff.; Trude Weiss-Rosmarin, *The Hebrew Moses* (New York, 1939) and "Moses on the Freudian Couch," *Jewish Spectator*, April 1973.

45. Simon Bernfeld, *The Foundations of Jewish Ethics*, 2d ed., trans. from the German by A. H. Koller (New York, 1968); Richard G. Hirsch, "Toward a Theology for Social Action," in *Judaism and Ethics*, ed. Daniel Jeremy Silver (New York, 1970), pp. 251–61.

46. Louis Finkelstein, *Jewish Self-Government in the Middle Ages*, 2d ed. (New York, 1964).

SELECTED BIBLIOGRAPHY

Davis, Moshe. *Beit Yisrael ba-Americah*. Jerusalem: Jewish Theological Seminary of America, 1970.

Dushkin, Alexander, and Engelman, Uriah. *Jewish Education in the United States*. 1969.

Fishman, Joshua. *Yiddish in America*. Bloomington: Indiana University, 1965.

Glanz, Rudolf. *Jews in Relation to the Cultural Milieu of the Germans in America*. New York, 1971.

Lurie, Harry L. *A Heritage Affirmed: The Jewish Federation Movement in America*. Philadelphia: Jewish Publication Society, 1961.

Neusner, Jacob. *American Judaism: Adventure in Modernity*. Englewood Cliffs, N. J.: Prentice-Hall, 1972.

The Social Tradition of the American Jew

MANHEIM S. SHAPIRO

JEWS CAME TO AMERICA at various times and from various places. In each land of origin, from each particular history or experience, they had acquired habits, outlooks, predispositions, and aspirations that differed from each other, in one respect or many. Each group of immigrants also found a different America (think, for example, of the America of 1664, of 1830, of 1880, or of 1920), and each proceeded to achieve some balance in the adjustment of what they were looking for to what they found; and to the extent they could, they engaged in the effort to shape what they found to their vision of the good life they were seeking.

They have been, therefore, a group of groups rather than a group. They have not been, like some of the other ethnic groups which arrived in this country, homogeneous in background and customs. Nor did they pursue a single course over time or in social space.

The task, then, in attempting to discuss the social "tradition" of American Jews, is to endeavor to trace out what has been, in fact, consistent and continuous for this entity we call "American Jewry"; to see what common strands we can find in the courses followed by segments of American Jewry. For "tradition" implies that which is transmitted from one generation to another, that which remains a common core for all those who bear the label, and that which, even when modified in the process, maintains some continuity among past, present, and future.

We discover that such transmission was not only chronologically vertical—that is, sequential in time—but also horizontal, from group to group at the same time. As the groups of Jews with differing social patterns met and mingled—or even remained socially distant from each other—they interacted with and influenced each other,

23

modifying each other's perceptions of themselves, of America, and of the norms of attitude, ideology, and behavior.[1]

To do all this effectively, we shall have to whittle away at some of the mythologies that have emerged with time. We shall have to examine some of the popularly held assumptions and images that may be satisfying or just plausible but also somewhat less than real. As only one example, we may note the seemingly trivial notion that "Jewish food"—the *gefuelte* fish, the chicken soup, the kosher pastrami or pickle, the lox or the borscht—is, in fact, characteristically Jewish. The truth is that this diet is a melange of East European, Baltic, and Southeast European foods, adopted or adapted by Jews from those countries, who brought these tastes and food habits with them, and who, perhaps because they were the most numerous component in Jewish immigration, were able to establish the popular notion that these were indeed characteristically "Jewish" foods. Yet to a "traditional" Middle Eastern or North African Jew, these dietary inclinations were totally alien. It is notable that until recently, when Israel began catering to American tourists, American Jewish tourists in Israel, where food habits have been more characteristically Middle Eastern, were frequently heard to complain that one couldn't get "a good Jewish meal" in Israel.

The point of this illustration is that such particular cultural patterns, expanded into generalizations, have been common in many areas of the development of the Jewish group in America. They have affected everything from liturgical patterns to occupational choices, from ideologies to leisure-time activities. It will be incumbent upon us, therefore, to attempt to distinguish between the cliches of what is "authentically" Jewish and the realities of what Jews have been, and thought, and done, and striven for.

We shall also have to recognize that there were a multiplicity of factors determining what was discarded and what was retained and passed on. The choices, calculating or accidental or covert, were affected by culture and by economics, by historical events, by political conditions, by technological developments, by leadership or scholarship, by the host of factors which influence human social development.

We shall consider a selected number of categories which seem to embody that which has indeed been "traditional" in the social development of American Jews.

We must begin, of course, with the historical background common to all Jews. That history included a great religious tradition, incorporated in a body of literature: Bible, Talmud, responsa, and commentaries. That literature contained not only a revolutionary and evolutionary concept of God and of a special relationship between the Jewish people and God but also a corpus of law, guides for behavior and for social relationships. Wherever they may have come from and however detailed their knowledge of that system, all Jews were aware of its existence and of its significance. Even when they deviated from its precepts or when Judaic authorities modified them to conform to new or necessary conditions, it was against that standard that the deviations and the modifications emerged. And whatever may have been the piety or the lack of it, much of the social behavior of Jews, both as Jews and as humans, was affected by patterns related to that body of doctrine and of prescription.

Thus, while for many Jews the Passover feast may have become a social event rather than a religious one (and an overwhelming majority of American Jews do still participate in a Passover feast),[2] the fact remains that the occasion is associated with religio-historical ideas. Even those rationalists who may reject as irrational the miracles described in the Passover Haggadah are nevertheless participating in an event, in some rituals, in the ingestion of certain foods and the abstention from others, which have all been prescribed by or connected with a religious tradition.

The religious tradition of American Jews is covered elsewhere in this volume, and we avoid any elaborate discussion of the subject here. But two points must be made about religion insofar as it affects social elements.

The first is that the awareness of the religion was a base upon which other attitudes and proclivities could more easily be erected.[3] Thus, notions of social equality and freedom, while they were also rooted in self-interest and in the creed of America, could arise more easily in those who had annually recited the ringing passage in the Passover Haggadah, "We were slaves in Egypt"; and for whom this concept was underlined by a later passage which tells us to instruct our children that it was not "they" but "we" who were liberated. Similarly, "Zionism," however the United Nations majority may seek to define it, is a viable impulse for a people which over many centuries has concluded each annual reading of the Haggadah (and of other liturgies) with the slogan, "Next year in Jerusalem." For that represented not merely a political statement but also a reminder of God's pledge to His people and a promise of the better ultimate world to come.

The second is that religious tendencies and organization, like various other forms of organization, were often, perhaps mostly, associated with social factors rather than with doctrinal choices. In America, the particular matter of the selection of a congregation was, and for many still is, a reflection of such factors as class and economic status, distance from the immigrant generations and the origins of the immigrant forebears, perceptions of "kind" (the sense of the social context in which one "belonged" or not), the neighborhood in which one lived, level of general education, and views of what is appropriate to America and to modernity. (In some of our studies of Jews in American cities, we found that attitudes on subjects such as "what makes a good Jew" were divided not only along lines of the branch of Judaism with which the respondents were affiliated, but also, in parallel divisions, along lines of whether both the respondent's parents were born in the United States or whether the respondent had at least one foreign-born parent, and similarly among those of different income levels.)[4]

Thus, a knowledge of a given Jew's congregational choice may be less an index to doctrinal preferences than to his social context, his perception of where he belongs in the world.[5] (As is also true, on another level, of whether he belongs to B'nai B'rith or the American Jewish Committee or the American Jewish Congress or the Jewish War Veterans. This may be less an indication of choice among differing prospectus ideologies and varying techniques of social action than one of social style and of the sense of position in social space. These affiliations, therefore, were often perceived as way-stations along the path of upward mobility, of having "made it" or not.)

Jewish immigration to America tended to occur in "waves"; that is, during particular periods, the Jewish immigrants tended to be largely (though not wholly) from particular geographical regions or of particular types. Thus, until after the American Revolution, most of the Jews who came to America were Sephardim, groups descended from the Jews who had been expelled from Spain in 1492 and from Portugal a few years later. Those Jews settled in the Netherlands, in England, and around the Mediterranean basin. But after the discovery of the New World some of them made their way to the new colonies of Holland, France, and England.

From the early 1800s to around 1870, most Jewish immigrants were from the German states and contiguous Central European countries. From 1870 to 1924, the East European Jews from Russia, Poland, the Baltic countries of Lithuania and Latvia, and Southeastern Europe predominated. From the 1930s through the early 1950s, most Jewish immigrants were either fleeing Hitler or were survivors of the Hitler Holocaust.[6]

There were, however, a number of social phenomena that were consistent for almost all these groups, with certain exceptions. Until the most recent immigrants, those who migrated to America tended to be the least "settled" of the Jews in their countries of origin. Those who were "haves," who had an economic or social position with some security or continuing prospects, stayed where they were. The ones who left were the ones who had the least to lose, or the adventurous to whom the new lands beckoned an opportunity to better themselves.

The first group of Jewish immigrants, actually refugees fleeing the Portuguese conquest of Recife in Brazil, cast ashore in Nieuw Amsterdam by a French ship's captain, encountered strong resistance to their permanent settlement there from Peter Stuyvesant. They were enabled to remain by the intervention of the established Jewish burghers in Amsterdam, who had sufficient status, power, and investment in the Dutch West India Company to be able to influence the decision. It is noteworthy, however, that the influential Jews were in Amsterdam, not in Nieuw Amsterdam.

The Germanic Jews who arrived here in the first two-thirds of the nineteenth century were largely those who were responding to the lack of economic opportunity in the German states or to the political and social repression which followed the failures of the revolutions of 1830 and 1848. The estimate that ninety percent of these German Jewish immigrants began their lives in America as peddlers is an index to the lack of capital with which they arrived. And for the over 1,500,000 East European Jewish immigrants who arrived here between 1880 and 1920, the figures indicate that they arrived here with per capita assets of nine dollars. Even those who fled Hitler in the 1930s were impelled to do so as they saw Jews deprived of jobs, or confronted with boycotts and expropriations, or harassed to the point where it became clear that there was no future for them. Some hung on until it was too late.

This was consistent, too. The few Jews who had been able, by virtue of particular successes, to win exemptions from tsarist restrictions against Jews, to gain wealth, to obtain permission to reside in the major cities of Moscow and St. Petersburg, tended to remain in Russia until the revolution of 1917 made it impossible for them to survive as bourgeoisie. Readers who saw the film, *The Garden of the Finzi-Contini*, will recall the inability of a wealthy Jewish family in Italy to believe that Fascism was directed at them, even to the moment of transportation.

The Jews who came to America, then, tended to be those who faced restriction, oppression, or actual physical violence in their country of origin. Certainly the "dream" of America beckoned to them on grounds of social ideology. The "American creed" coincided with prophetic visions of a world where all men would be treated with justice and where the strong would share with the weak. But it also took a certain desperation and a certain readiness for risk-taking actually to move people to migrate.

It also took a certain kind of raw courage and self-reliance. To steal across borders in Europe, to travel thousands of miles across the sea in frail vessels, to land in a foreign country with no knowledge of the language and little more than the clothes on one's back, demanded a drive and a fortitude that must command admiration. What is more to the point, the same drives continued after arrival in this country.[7]

Jews in America have, on the whole, been "successful"; that is to say, either they or their children were able to move up the economic ladder. They did this in a number of ways.

To begin with, many of these Jews brought with them talents which were in tune with the economic needs of America. Those peddlers of the first two-thirds of the nineteenth century served as a vital link in providing the settlers who were expanding along the American frontier with the goods necessary for the maintenance of a relatively civilized way of life. Whether it was needles, buttons, and yard goods, or clothing, or seed and tools, the peddler was in the early days a significant contributor to the expansion of the nation. Many of those on the Eastern seaboard were engaged in the early days in import and export. As those who began with peddling gained sufficient capital, they established stores at a crossroads or a small town, and their businesses grew with the newly established later-to-be-major cities. It is of more than passing coincidence that most of the major cities of the Midwest, the South, and the Far West were founded precisely during the period when the Germanic Jewish immigrants were arriving, 1830–70. Hence the explanation for the "Jewish" names of so many major department stores in so many of these cities.

It is notable that immigrant Jews, with only rare exceptions, did not become farmers. This was inherent in their economic history. Having come largely from countries where Jews had for centuries been forbidden to hold land, farming was not one of their skills. For the most part, they had been confined to economic functions, such as trading and management or artisanship; these were the areas of possibility they brought with them. In Poland, for example, Jews had been "imported" centuries earlier to serve as middle-men between the aristocracy and the peasantry in the absence of a middle class. They had served as tavern-keepers, tax and rent collectors, and stewards for the large landholders. As the Jewish population grew, they also became small traders, merchants in market towns, and artisans (tailors, carpenters, house painters) in the towns and villages where they were permitted to live. Furthermore, they were literate, accustomed to dealing with ideas and with figures. Their background had equipped them with skills and experience for economic functions which were needed in America. They tended, in the early days, to concentrate in the distributive and service trades and industries rather than in manufacturing or extractive industries.

Of course, there were exceptions. Those individual Jews who were able to accumulate large amounts of capital might invest in copper-mining or in the acquisition of land, but by and large their tendency was to enter those fields which involved the management of trade, of risk, and of intellectual services.

The century of 1870 to 1970 is a period of special interest. In 1870 there were about 250,000 Jews in the United States. By 1920 there were around 2,500,000, an increase produced primarily by the immigration of East European Jews. They differed from their predecessors in a number of ways.

To begin with, they tended to cluster in the Eastern seaboard port cities: New York, Philadelphia, Boston, Baltimore. There were two reasons for this: first of all, they could form colonies of those who were familiar to them, other Jews who spoke the same language, ate the same foods, shared similar memories. Secondly, arriving without capital dictated a need for employment; this was most possible where there were friends, and where there was opportunity for jobs in trades or industries for which the immigrant was equipped. In these large metropolitan areas it was possible to obtain employment in light industry (garment manufacture, as one example); or in commercial enterprises; or, when capital became available, to open a small grocery, butcher shop, stationery store, or dry goods store (it might require the step from pushcart peddling to a fixed location, but if one bought and sold well, the transition could be made); or to find opportunity as an artisan (for instance, as a tailor, carpenter, or painter). In addition, the chances to find intellectual and cultural stimulation were greater for this intellectually oriented group in the large metropolitan areas.

The East European Jews in the metropolitan areas, then, were able to take advantage not only of the educational and cultural opportunities available in the general society (from night classes in public schools to colleges and universities; from concerts to theater; from newspapers to free public libraries), but they also were able to create their own theater, amateur and professional; establish a press of newspapers and other periodicals; form debating societies and political groups. In short, in these locations there was a sufficiently large population of those with similar backgrounds to create a world which softened the shock of transplantation and made adjustment easier.[8]

What was consistent for these as for other Jewish immigrant groups, however, was the drive not only for upward socio-economic mobility per se, but also the drive to enter entrepreneurial and professional occupations.

And Jews in America have been remarkably successful in achieving this aspiration. From peddler to established merchant was an already familiar pattern by 1870. But it is also true that what was numerically a predominantly wage-earning group in 1925 is now predominantly engaged in ownership and management, sales, professions, and white-collar occupations. For the East European immigrants (indeed for all Jewish immigrants), the jump from laboring or proletarian class to middle class was generally made in one generation. The garment industry, in which in the 1930s most of the workers were Jews, may now have a majority of its owners and managers as Jews (except for those enterprises which have been absorbed into major corporate structures), but certainly only a small minority of its workers are Jews. Jews are still officials and managers of the major unions in this industry, but almost none of the rank and file members are Jewish. Notably, in virtually no case did the son of a worker in the garment industry follow his father into the shop.

The father worked hard and long either to become an entrepreneur in the industry, or to enable his children to become something else—a doctor, a lawyer, an accountant, a teacher, a manager, a scientist, a writer or musician.

In achieving these goals, Jews had two factors going for them—their background was suited to what was happening in the American society and economy, and they used what was the principal ladder for upward mobility, education. There are numerous speculative explanations offered for this phenomenon. It is suggested that the emphasis upon the education of one's children is one. The fact that such occupations were closed to Jews until relatively recently in their countries of origin is another. The notion that being one's own boss or a "free" professional immunizes one to the possible restrictive impact of an anti-Semitic employer is still another. And the meaning to people with a group memory of attack and forced migration of the portability of economic assets consisting of marketable skills or knowledge is a fourth.

Whatever the reasons, the process was real. Parents vied with each other over their children's achievements in school. Jewish children consistently attended school for longer periods of time than the averages for the general population. The Jewish adult population has a higher proportion of college graduates than the general population and than that of virtually every other religious denomination, with the possible exception of the Episcopalians. The occupational and income shifts conform to what is suggested by this description of educational achievement. Proportionately, as has been suggested earlier, the Jewish group also has more professionals and managers than do other comparable groups. Consequently, studies show that Jews have a higher per capita income than either Catholics or Protestants. (These are, of course, gross figures. Protestant figures, for example, are lower because the averages include most of the blacks and most of the rural population.)[9]

Lest these statements leave a false impression, it should be stated that there are still hundreds of thousands of poor Jews. However, these tend to be the elderly, the foreign-born and the less well educated, categories which, incidentally, tend to overlap.

To facilitate the processes of adjustment and adaptation to the new society, Jews tended to organize themselves and their institutions in ways which would reinforce these possibilities. Even organizations and institutions intended to conserve traditional Judaic commitments and practices tended to accommodate to the American scene in ways which made both the institution and its adherents more American in style and tone. This was a process which had been going on for many centuries as Jews moved from place to place; the American adaptation was only a continuation, not a sharply new development.

To take only one illustration, the institution and practices of the rabbinate changed in ways which made the American rabbi ultimately much more like an American Protestant minister than the rabbi-scholar of East European Jewry, or the French *rabbin*, who tended to be more like a Catholic hierarch and after Napoleon a government-related functionary, or the English rabbi, who tended to manifest characteristics similar to those of an Anglican priest or curate. There were, of course, differences in content—in theology and in liturgy—but the overt style and the relationship to the congregation became similar to those of the minister or preacher.

Organization began, however, around the religious functions. In the pre-revolutionary period it generally began with the formation of an association to acquire land for a Jewish burial ground, both because Jews wanted to be buried with Jewish ritual and because, as nonbelievers, they were denied access to Christian cemeteries, which as often as not were in churchyards. To a devout Jew, burial alongside graves whose headstones bore crosses or other Christological figures and symbols was unthinkable. One notes that one of the many brushes between the small group of Jews that had settled in Nieuw Amsterdam and Governor Peter Stuyvesant was over the right to acquire land for burial. The next step was for these groups to form a congregation. For the Sephardic Jews, with their experience of Holland or England, the congregation was not only the vehicle for worship and prayer, it was also *the* community.[10]

It was a social body in the sense that by participating in it a Jew was not only enrolling himself in a system for religious services and practices but also demonstrating his adherence to the Jewish group. On the informal level, Jews frequently found in the congregation a center for the making and maintenance of friendships, an arena in which their children might find suitable Jewish marriage-partners and adults sources for help when they needed it.

Such help was forthcoming (as when a cargo was lost in a storm at sea or in an Indian raid, or when there were "family troubles" like illness or accident) both from individuals and, fairly soon, in a formal way from the congregation itself. Congregations established funds administered by a committee of prominent members, in confidence, to assist the needy widows and orphans of deceased members and ultimately also to such members as had themselves fallen on hard times. By the early nineteenth century, these congregational functions had been extended to provide assistance to needy Jewish families or to transient Jews who were not members of the congregation. They also became the matrix out of which emerged Jewish orphanages, free Jewish schools for the children of Jewish families who could not provide tuition, and homes for the Jewish aged.

By the time of the Revolution there were active congregations in such places as New York, Philadelphia, Newport, Charleston, and Savannah. As the Jewish population increased and settled in additional areas of the country, the number of congregations also increased. Through the first third of the nineteenth century at least, the congregation remained the sole center for Jewish affiliation.

It is of more than passing interest (to this writer, at any rate) that there appear to have been few if any conflicts arising out of the shift of the preponderance of Jewry in America from those of Sephardic origin to those of Germanic origin. The Central European Jews seem to have joined the Sephardic congregations, to have been fully accepted, and to have accepted the liturgical practices of the Sephardic group. At some time, as the German Jews began to out-number their Sephardic co-religionists, changes occurred, but these changes appear to have occurred as an evolution rather than as a resolution of conflict.

This may, of course, have been due to the fact that with acculturation, the original Sephardic Jewish families were also assimilating and abandoning their Jewish commitments. Indeed, it is not possible to find descendants of the original Jewish settlers in Nieuw Amsterdam who are still Jewish. The substantial numbers of Sephardic Jews in America today represent a much later Sephardi immigration, after World War I, not the descendants of the pre-revolutionary settlers.

It is a significant fact that beginning in those early days, it did become a major tradition of American Jewry to provide for and assist new Jewish settlers. Sometimes, there were some who opposed additional Jewish immigration, whose assistance may have been tinged with hostility, or who may have been involved in culture conflicts or mutually unfavorable stereotypes; but the assistance was forthcoming nevertheless.

Of course, this was a tradition of many centuries' standing.

Biblical and talmudic injunctions are replete with commands to care for the widowed, the orphaned, and the deprived; to welcome the "stranger in thy gates"; and to rescue the hostage and the refugee. Centuries of experience in Europe, where Jews were denied access to the facilities and services of the general community, and where they had to rely upon each other for security and for access to the foods and practices shared only by other Jews, had inculcated in communities of Jews both the habits and procedures for such mutual support.

Even those who were opposed to additional Jewish immigration found that the very reasons for their opposition impelled the same assistance. Whether it was the fear that Jews might become a public charge or that the alien-seemingness of new immigrants might provoke anti-Jewish sentiment or discrimination, providing assistance to self-support, to adjustment, and, indeed, to adaptation would allay the very fears of opponents. For such aid, by its nature and character, was "Americanizing" in effect, whether calculatingly so or only incidental to the techniques for enabling the new resident to manage effectively in the new society.

As the number of German Jews increased, they also brought with them additional modes of organizing, outside the orbit of the synagogue or the congregation. B'nai B'rith, a "fraternal order," was organized in 1843 by a number of German Jews to provide a "secular" vehicle for Jewish interests. Having been among the first Jews to be "emancipated," during the Napoleonic era, the German Jews had adapted to their new status by making the distinction between the "religious" and the "secular." It was their philosophical position that Jews were citizens of the nations in which they lived, distinguished only by a difference in religion from their fellow-citizens of those nations. This fit well into the American pattern, in which religion was considered a private matter and in which, therefore, difference of religion was the most acceptable form of differentness. Reinforced by later developments, this led, however, to an organizational separation between "religious" and "secular" Jewish organizations. This was a phenomenon stimulated by numerous forces: the influence of the eighteenth- and nineteenth-century revolutions in thought and politics which espoused the separation of church and state, of religious and secular; the exposure of Jews to the rationalist education encouraged by such movements; and, as the division of Jews into "branches of Judaism" grew, the effort to provide services and associations in which Jews of every persuasion could cross denominational lines.

In any case, there developed, from what had been congregation-centered assistance programs to the widowed and orphaned, the unfortunate, the aged, and the transient, a vast network of social services. In addition there arose organizations and institutions designed to provide association with others of similar background (people from a particular town, region, or country or origin); mutual assistance organizations (burial societies, insurance or "free loan" societies); organizations to express commonly held views of Jews or groups of Jews on social issues, or the "interests" of Jewry as a whole; recreational and educational bodies; and organizations to mobilize Jewish opinion on political and ideological positions, whether on issues of specific Jewish interest like Zionism, or a general view of desirable social structure like socialism or civil rights and civil liberties.

There were several different kinds of sequences involved in the process of development, beginning with direct assistance to the deprived by the advantaged and moving to the provision of services which would enable the disadvantaged to make their own way (like baby health-care centers, classes in citizenship or occupational training), to services which assisted in individual and family adjustment (counseling, vocational guidance, family guidance), and to providing vehicles for self-adjustment and for the development of skills and activities which would enrich life. Another kind of sequence was from service by volunteers to service by professionals with policy and resources provided by the volunteers.

Still another sequence was from the discrete organization or agency, supported by a particular interest in that form of service, to communitywide or even nationwide consolidated and coordinated fund-raising and planning systems. Where initially funds had been solicited for a particular organization or institution—let us say, a home for the aged or a Jewish hospital—beginning in the 1880s, there developed the institution known as the "federation" of a given community. The federation raised money from all the Jews in the town for all or most of the service agencies, and then allocated funds to the various agencies according to some concept of the order of priorities in the minds of the board of the federation, or the contesting claims of those who could wield power in the decision-making, either by virtue of their stature or (more likely, though the two may be interlocking) by virtue of the magnitude of their contributions to the communal fund. It is to be presumed as well that in some way these decisions reflected the priorities of the Jewish community, even if there were sometimes those who were disgruntled by a given decision. Given that the entire apparatus was voluntary, the system could not have survived repeated decisions that outraged the will or the interests of the majority of the community's citizens.

Simultaneously with the growth of the federations to plan and to raise funds for local service organizations, there arose community "welfare funds" to raise money for national and overseas services. What often began as individual philanthropy (as, for example, to assist Jews overseas who were deprived as a result of governmental, social, and economic conditions), ultimately became a much broader appeal to the general Jewish public, and decision-making became more widely dispersed as support was secured from a greater segment of the Jewish population.

Still another form of organization developed in the larger cities after the massive influx of the Jewish immigration on both sides of the turn of the century. The normal pattern was for the established Jews to provide services both for immigration and after arrival for the adjustment of the immigrant. And this was true then, too. There were, however, significant differences between the two groups. The new arrivals were Yiddish-speaking, Orthodox or nonreligiously radical; the older residents were none of these. Certainly, those in positions of power in the service agencies tended to be German in origin, Reform, English-speaking, and politically conservative to moderate. The immigrants were predominantly working class, the established residents primarily professionals or entrepreneurs. But what was perhaps the most striking difference were the mutual perceptions of each other. The newcomers saw many of the indigenous Jewish leaders as "assimilated" or "assimilating," that is to say, having abandoned the ways of their fathers; looking, acting, talking, and even praying "like Goyim"; and what is more, insisting that they were "Americans of the Hebrew faith" rather than Jews who happened to be in America. To the established Jewish community, the East European immigrants often seemed obstinately alien, old-fashioned, and dangerously unwilling to modify their immigrant attitudes and ideologies.

Hence, while the agencies and federations of the established Jewish communities in America did provide help to the East European Jews (agencies were often, in fact, established for precisely this purpose), there nevertheless emerged frictions and resentment. In a number of communities, there sprang up "downtown" federations which represented, for the most part, the East European immigrants and which competed with the "uptown" federations, the vehicle of the established philanthropists. The "downtown" federations were, in a sense, the "do-it-yourself" social services of the East European Jews.

There was certainly some justification for the feelings of the East European Jews. For the social agencies, in their helping functions, were, in fact, "Americanizing." A baby health center that taught mothers new ways of feeding and clothing their infants, or a neighborhood center teaching tenement-area teenagers to play basketball or adults to speak and write English, was modifying culture. Of course, the agencies and organizations of the "downtown" federations also turned out to be "Americanizing" or Westernizing in their effect. Whatever the extent to which they represented loyalties and nostalgia for a vanishing Old World culture, whatever their stated aims to conserve that culture, whatever the ideological differences with other benefactors, Americanization was what their constituencies wanted. They might conduct their meetings in Yiddish or organize into labor unions or socialist clubs, but they also served as the means for their constituents and clients to adjust to a new world. It might be that the tone was different, that it was more "comfortable" for these people to work out the adjustment under the aegis of the more familiar atmosphere of those who thought and talked as they did, but the long-run results were the same.[11]

"Emancipation" for the Central and West European Jews and migration for the East European Jews both produced a similar effect, a grasping of the opportunity to achieve equality and freedom and access to those aspects of social and economic life which had been denied them under restrictive or oppressive regimes. Therefore, it often seemed to these Jews that both equality and upward mobility required them to divest themselves of qualities and traits which might cause them to stand out from other Americans in unacceptably different ways. While the established Jews might fear that foreign-seeming Jews would unleash a wave of anti-Semitism, the newer immigrants saw the same differences as a possible block to progress or achievement. In part, they Westernized themselves, in dress, in language, and in attitude. More importantly, they pushed their children to learn and adopt the new culture and the new style of life through education in the public schools and on up to colleges and universities, through the encouragement of new standards of expectation and behavior, and through institutional patterns which reinforced the new kind of life-style.

The vast East European Jewish immigration came to a sudden stop in 1924, when the first United States immigration-quota laws went into effect. By the time of World War II, less than a generation later, most of the differences described above had been wiped out. The "downtown" federations and the "uptown" federations had merged. In addition, the trend to the merger of federations and welfare funds into a single community-wide organization for the systematization of support and planning for Jewish causes was well under way. (Today, even in the few cities where there are still separate entities called federation and welfare fund, the distinction is often technical and the two bodies may have the same executive director and either the same board or interlocking ones.)

What is more, social intercourse and marriage between the two groups became possible and common. Leadership in federations, in social or communal organizations and services, became integrated; where the helping services had at one time rested almost exclusively in the hands of the families of German Jewish immigrants (except in the indigenous organizations of East European Jews), they were gradually integrated. The economic stature of representatives of the two groups became more equal. The gaps in the level of general education narrowed or disappeared.

None of these changes occurred overnight or dramatically. In the 1950s and 1960s, when this writer directed several studies of the attitudes of Jews in different American communities, we found that Reform Jews were more likely to regard family service agencies and hospitals as more important Jewish causes, while Conservative Jews were more likely to favor Jewish education and aid to Israel. These were, of course, social distinctions rather than religious, doctrinal ones. They represented differences of family affiliation and orientation more than they represented differences in religious viewpoint.

Or, to take another example, in the period immediately after World War II, when the establishment of a "Jewish homeland" in Palestine was at issue, Reform Jews, who opposed a definition of Jewry as a nation rather than as the affiliates of a particular religion, could nevertheless find themselves in a position similar to that of political Zionists, with the exception that they arrived at that position through a "philanthropic" impulse to provide a haven for the survivors of the Hitler Holocaust. Practically, however, the positions were the same. Some of the very people who had been vigorous advocates of an "anti-state" position could voice pride in having been instrumental in Israel's establishment and survival.

The differences have, by and large, disappeared. (It should be noted, however, that in many ways, the German Jews who fled from Hitler before and after World War II repeated the experience of earlier and larger waves of immigration except that it was the East European contingent who were now the benefactors, and the Germans who were the recipients.) But the penchant for organizing has not changed. The *American Jewish Year Book* lists over 350 "national" Jewish organizations. These are cultural and educational, overseas aid, community relations and social action, religious, or coordinating bodies for the others. Were we to try to guess at a figure which would include all the local branches of national membership organizations, the federations, the local synagogues and their satellite bodies like brotherhoods and sisterhoods, the service agencies like family service societies, Jewish community centers (and the clubs or groups organized within the centers), vocational guidance agencies, sheltered workshops, schools and adult education programs, and others, the estimate of the total would number well into the thousands.

In part, this phenomenon has historical roots in the periods when Jews, isolated from the general community, had to develop their own facilities for communal functions. In part, it is attributable to the American pattern of voluntary organization. In part, it represents a sense among Jews that if they do not take care of their own and of themselves, nobody else will. In part, also, it is related to a sense among Jews that the essence of being Jewish is the feeling of connectedness to other Jews and that "belonging" to something is a concrete way of acting out this sense of connection.

It is a continuous and consistent tradition of American Jews to respond to the needs and difficulties of Jews elsewhere. For three-quarters of a century, the American Joint Distribution Committee has provided aid and succor to Jews in need in all parts of the world. ORT (Organization for Rehabilitation and Training) has established vocational training programs, initially for Jews but more recently for others as well, in over fifty countries. HIAS (Hebrew Immigrant Aid Society) has helped Jews in transit, in forced or voluntary migration, to find entry into a new home and to establish themselves once there.[12]

It would be inappropriate to engage here in an extended discussion of the uniqueness of a religion which incorporates a sense of peoplehood in its religious teachings. The Covenant was made not with "believers" alone but with all the descendants of Abraham, Isaac, and Jacob. There can be no doubt, however, of the depth of feeling among Jews that they share a common fate as well as a common faith. That feeling is most vigorously touched when Jews someplace are under attack, in jeopardy, or suffering from oppression. This was manifest in the response of American Jews to the pogroms and other attacks and restrictions inflicted upon Jews in the last half-century of tsarist rule in Russia, as it is today in response to the treatment of Jews in the Soviet Union.

It is most manifest in the support of almost all American Jews for Israel. Although, as has been suggested earlier, there were at one time numbers of Jews in America who were in principle opposed to the doctrines of Zionism and to the establishment of a Jewish state, there is today a statistically negligible minority who articulate doubts of the need for Israel to survive or for all Jews to be concerned about that survival. With the memory of the Holocaust still fresh in the minds of Jews, there is a sense among many, perhaps most, American Jews that in a world which would permit the Jews of Israel, or Israel itself, to be destroyed, no Jew could face the future with security.

All these organizational and mutual assistance efforts have, of course, cost money. American Jews have been remarkably generous in this respect. Millions upon millions of dollars have been raised and expended for these purposes. In some degree, again, this is related to the obligation of *tzedakah* (which translates poorly as "charity" since it also incorporates, etymologically, elements of "righteousness" and "justice"). There is no tithing in contemporary Judaism, but studies reveal that Jews tend to give larger amounts and larger proportions of their income to "charitable" causes in almost every category than do the members of other religious groups in America.

These acts of *tzedakah* extend beyond the specifically Jewish causes to all appeals for generosity. While Jews tend to give by far more of their contributions to Jewish causes, they also tend to be more generous than their neighbors in gifts to general community campaigns like Red Feather drives or the various medical research programs or programs for civil rights and civil liberties, legal aid programs, or programs to achieve equality or assistance to the disadvantaged.

Jews in America have always been involved with such efforts for a multiplicity of reasons. For one thing, as suggested, the prophetic visions of a good and a just society still reverberate in the psyche of the Jew. However removed from the teachings themselves any individual may be, the culture of the group embodies these concepts. For another, the open and the just society seems to hold out more hope for the Jew himself than does the authoritarian one. Jews in America have tended to align themselves with "liberal" social views in America precisely because, in addition to the abstract concepts of what a society ought to be like, the position of Jews tended to seem, and often is, more advantageous in an open society than in a hierarchical or authoritarian one.

The opportunities for Jews were dependent to a substantial degree upon the images of the Jew in the mind of his neighbors. As was also the case with blacks, America, through most of its history, suffered a conflict between creed and deed with respect to Jews. The resistance of Peter Stuyvesant to the settlement of Jews in Nieuw Amsterdam has already been mentioned. In his correspondence with the Dutch West India Company, he used such phrases as "the deceitful race—such hateful enemies and blasphemers of the name of Christ."

In popular novels of the first half of the nineteenth century, Jews were likely to be described in such terms as "greedy vultures . . . scrambling for the scattered remnants of ruined fortunes." Not only their characters were described in such unfavorable terms, but also their appearances. They tended to be described as hook-nosed, bearded, and uncannily mysterious in visage and comportment.[13]

In short, just as Jews had brought a culture with them, so too had Christian immigrants. And that culture included centuries of the "teaching of contempt," in the telling phrase of Jules Isaac. The consequences of such memories were often restriction, hostility, and discrimination.

Jews were, therefore, in an organized way, engaged throughout their history in America in attempts to correct these aberrant views in the minds of other Americans, to eliminate quotas in colleges and universities, to nullify restrictive covenants in the sale of homes, to reduce job discrimination, and to facilitate mutual acceptance among Americans. Almost never did Jews fight these battles or wage these struggles solely for Jews; on the contrary, they tended to engage themselves in these matters on the ground that "*all* men are created equal." They allied themselves with constitutional principles, with social justice, and with the disabilities of members of other racial, religious, and ethnic groups in this country.[14]

The slogan for this effort was "individual merit." That is to say, most Jewish organizations engaged in the field of community relations espoused the notion that the individual should be free to move in the society as far as his native talents and his efforts to advance himself could take him. It denied "race, religion, or national origin" as a sufficient cause for any form of distinction or discrimination. By and large, these efforts served both Jews and America as a whole well. Over the years artificial barriers have been reduced. Schools, occupations, access to housing, opportunities for self-advancement have been broadened.

There were, however, a number of dilemmas attached to this process. For many Jews, this egalitarian ideal led also to the conclusion that group identifications themselves led to the stereotyping, divisiveness, and discrimination which blighted the society. For many such, the ideal society seemed to be one in which all such differences, including their own, would disappear. Along with other trends, among some American Jews there has existed a tendency to abandon their Jewish connections and to disappear as Jews, whether by inanition or by calculated plan. By the 1950s, with the defeat of the most massive anti-Semitic campaign in world history, some Jews perceived the situation as an augury for that utopian world in which group distinctions would disappear.

This was balanced, greatly outweighed, by the opposing tendency of those for whom Hitlerism fanned the latent spark of Jewish consciousness; for whom the establishment, the existence, and indeed the tribulations of the State of Israel aroused these feelings. For still others, the more recent emphasis in American society as a whole upon the validity of loyalty to racial and ethnic consciousness and culture has intensified their examination and clarification of their own Jewishness and their Jewish commitments.

The loss, the seepage, the attenuation, during the processes of acculturation and accommodation, may all be related to the weakening of two major instrumentalities which had served Jewry in the maintenance of the group and of its mores and standards: the family and the community. Both had roots in the teachings of Judaism, but both also had been socially functional in the historical experiences of Jews. In a life of stress and apprehension and of constant danger (whether of physical attack or of explusion), the cohesive family provided a measure of physical and certainly psychological security. Children were indeed hostages to the future; and the availability of reliable nuclear and extended families provided a hedge against peril or disaster. When this was combined with precepts which governed the roles, relationships, and obligations of family members, the family and family life became a medium for the transmission of accepted behavior and of expected commitments.

Family and community interacted in the maintenance of the group and its norms. In the centuries when Jews lived in Europe, they tended to be isolated from the host communities in which they lived. The separation was both imposed and voluntarily maintained; imposed by hostile and repressive Christian societies; voluntarily maintained so Jews could continue their particular commitments to a life-system involving religiously ordained practices, including worship, study, standards of conduct, dietary controls, and a particular system of domestic and civic law. For those Jews there was no distinction between religious law and secular law. Secular law was outlined in the sacred books of law. And religious law also covered secular behavior: domestic relations, obligations of man to man, and systems for the governance of the community.

In such close-knit communities, the community could impose standards of conduct because it could also impose sanctions, whether by as formal a procedure as decision by a rabbi or a rabbinic court or as informal a technique as gossip and the known expectations of neighbors.

Each segment of Jewish immigrants brought such systems with it when it arrived in America. But migration, the physical move itself, already began to loosen ties. Living among non-Jewish neighbors, the propinquity to others, reduced the cohesiveness of Jews as a community. In many instances, the Jews who arrived in this country arrived as individuals. Those immigrant Jewish peddlers who roamed the country were only rarely in contact with other Jews. And the drive toward Americanization, the effort to be like rather than unlike, established new standards and reduced old commitments.

For a generation or two each Old Country system persisted. Jews even to this day are less likely than the general population to dissolve marriages through divorce, less prone to alcoholism, more likely to provide for longer periods of schooling for their children, and so on.

But as the stream of immigration thinned out, as acculturation proceeded, Jews also became more likely to suffer the effects of changes in the society at large. Hence, as industrialization proceeded, as urbanization grew, as bureaucratization and specialization and alienation spread, Jews too were affected.

Jews became much more like the white middle class in America. With this came influences that affected the earlier bulwarks of Jewish transmission. Divorce became more prevalent. Family roles and relationships changed. The extended family disintegrated. The three-generation household disappeared. Children were reared for departure upon graduation from high school rather than for continuing relationship with the family. Even if Jews tended to form Jewish neighborhoods, these areas were not homogeneously so and certainly lacked the potency of the old Jewish communities. Mobility attenuated Jewish community social controls still further. Propinquity and similarity and the dropping of bars on both sides made for an ever-increasing rate of intermarriage with non-Jews.[15]

Perhaps the most critical change of all was the adoption of the Christian categories of "religious" and "secular." For Judaism, the religion and teachings of a way of life, were no longer inherent in every aspect of daily living but became a "department" of life. Family life, which had been regulated by ritual and practice, now only exercised ceremony as an "activity" on a par with other activities like TV-viewing or going to the ball game. "Jewish" activities, whether synagogal or other-organizational, have become for many a form of leisure-time activity, of hobby, to which one devotes certain hours free from "major" and mundane obligations.

There are signs of revival. Every Jewish organization is applying itself to the restoration of the family—family counseling, family-life education, family retreats, programs for singles, for parents without partners, for divorced fathers and their children. Jewish education programs, both for children and for adults, formal and informal, proliferate. The sequence of each succeeding generation being "less" Jewish than its parents seems to have halted or slowed. Missions and trips to Israel seem for the most part to inspire a greater attachment to "the Jewish connection."

How durable or extensive any of these movements may be only history will tell.

Meanwhile, we do know this. In their history in America, Jews have made remarkable social adjustments. They have applied themselves with both diligence and skill to mastering the intricacies of accommodation to American society. They have, in turn, brought to bear on the shaping of American society their own heritage of social vision and social experience. This interaction will have a substantial impact upon the future both of America and of American Jews. The unfolding continues.

NOTES

1. See Charles S. Liebman, "Changing Characteristics of Orthodox, Conservative and Reform Jews," *Sociological Analysis*, 27 (Winter 1966): 210–12.

2. Marshall Sklare and Joseph Greenblum, *Jewish Identity on the Suburban Frontier* (New York: Basic Books, 1967), p. 52 et seq.

3. For a perceptive analysis of the relationships between Old Country cultures and the processes of acculturation, see Milton M. Gordon, *Assimilation in American Life* (New York: Oxford University Press, 1964).

4. The Southville Survey of Jewish Attitudes (1959), the Bayville Study of Jewish Attitudes (1961), the Kansas City Survey of Jewish Attitudes (1962), the Baltimore Survey of Jewish Attitudes (1963). All by Manheim S. Shapiro. Processed. Unpublished. In archives of American Jewish Committee, New York.

5. Liebman, op. cit.

6. Morris U. Schappes. *A Documentary History of the Jews in the United States; 1654–1875* (New York: Citadel Press, 1950), pp. 1–5.

7. The personal histories and processes of adjustment of numbers of such Jews are revealed by many of the memoirs included in Jacob R. Marcus, ed., *Memoirs of American Jews*, 3 vols. (Philadelphia: Jewish Publication Society, 1955).

8. Irving Howe, in *World of Our Fathers*, provides a detailed view of what the East European immigrants brought to America, what they created, and what they gave up. Irving Howe, with the assistance of Kenneth Libo, *World of Our Fathers* (New York: Harcourt Brace Jovanovich, 1976).

9. For summaries of statistical findings of the educational, economic, and other patterns of American Jews, see Manheim S. Shapiro, "The Sociology of Jewish Life," in *Meet the American Jew*, ed. Belden Menkus (Nashville: Broadman Press, 1963).

10. See the extended description of these processes in Joseph L. Blau, "The Spiritual Life of American Jewry," in *The Characteristics of American Jews*, ed. Nathan Glazer et al. (New York: Jewish Education Committee Press, 1965), pp. 72–77.

11. See Glazer et al., op. cit., pp. 168–72.

12. Ibid., pp. 183–85.

13. Louis Harap. *The Image of the Jew in American Literature* (Philadelphia: Jewish Publication Society, 1974). This volume contains extensive analysis and quotation of such descriptions on pp. 1–259.

14. See Albert Vorspan, "Jews and Social Justice," and Benjamin Kaplan, "Jews and Social Equality," in Menkus, op. cit.

15. See Victor D. Sanua, "Attitudes of Jewish Students Toward Intermarriage" (pp. 240–61), and Manheim S. Shapiro, "Intermarriage and the Community" (pp. 262–71), in *The Jewish Family in a Changing World*, ed. Gilbert S. Rosenthal (New York: Thomas Yoseloff, 1970).

SELECTED BIBLIOGRAPHY

Drachsler, Julius. *Democracy and Assimilation: The Blending of Immigrant Heritages in America*. New York: Macmillan Co., 1920.
Efron, Benjamin. *Currents and Trends in Contemporary Jewish Thought*. New York: Ktav, 1965.
Friedman, Lee M. *Pilgrims in a New Land*. Philadelphia: Jewish Publication Society, 1948.
Glazer, Nathan; Blau, Joseph L.; Stein, Herman D.; Handlin, Oscar; and Handlin, Mary F. *The Characteristics of American Jews*. New York: Jewish Education Committee Press, 1965.
Gordon, Milton. *Assimilation in American Life*. New York: Oxford University Press, 1964.
Greeley, Andrew M. *Ethnicity in the United States: A Preliminary Reconnaissance*. New York: John Wiley, 1974.
Liebman, Charles S. *The Ambivalent American Jew*. Philadelphia: Jewish Publication Society, 1973.
Sklare, Marshall. *America's Jews*. New York: Random House, 1971.
Stember, Charles Herbert, et al. *Jews in the Mind of America*. New York: Basic Books, 1966.

The Religious Tradition of the American Jew

ABRAHAM J. KARP

OBSERVERS OF contemporary Jewish religious life in America note two features which characterize the American Jewish community—its tripartite division into Orthodox-Conservative-Reform, and the centrality of the synagogue in Jewish life and activity. Religious denominationalism, to be sure, exists in other Jewish communities, and the synagogue has played and continues to play a central role in Jewish life, but nowhere to the extent and degree to which these obtain in America. Both of these features have their roots in American realities, and are the result of wedding Jewish needs to American possibilities. The climate of America, which made possible and gave legitimacy to division, also caused the Jew to organize his Jewish life in congregational form. The tripartite division and the synagogue need, then, to be considered in their American historical setting.

The Tripartite Religious Community: How It Came to Be

The American Jewish community is at one and the same time part of world Jewry and a component of the American nation. It is shaped and influenced by both. It responds to requirements placed upon it by Jewry and demands made of it by America.

The formative period of organized Jewish religious life in America is the century between the Congress of Vienna in 1815 and the outbreak of World War I in 1914. During that century the Jewish population in the United States increased a thousandfold from about twenty-five hundred to some two and one-half million. In 1815 there were some half-dozen congregations. By 1914 there was a religious community divided into Orthodox, Reform, and Conservative groupings, each with its rabbinic seminary, congregational union, and rabbinic organizations.

The European Jewish historical experience in that century was largely that of emancipation, enlightenment, and migration. The promise of the French Revolution of *Liberté, Egalité, Fraternité* was carried by Napoleon's conquering armies through Europe. Grudgingly, but increasingly, civic and political rights were extended to the Jew. The periods of reaction which followed the Congress of Vienna and the abortive revolutions of 1848 erased many hard-won rights, but not all. The Jew's usefulness to an expanding economy opened for him heretofore closed doors. He entered these with alacrity. He sensed that the price of admission was a lessening of Jewish national feelings and aspirations, and a casting off of the ways which made him distinct and distinguished.

These sentiments were fortified by his experience with enlightenment, the Jew's absorption of and integration in the general culture of the country and its civilization. Both in its West European form of *Jüdische Wissenschaft*, and in its East European expression, *Haskalah*, it led to loosening of ancestral ties, a broadening of cultural and spiritual experimentation, and a restructuring of communal forms and religious usage. In its extreme it led to apostasy, the baptismal certificate considered the ticket of admission to the world beyond the ghetto. But for the most it led to changes in synagogue and home ritual, a restatement of religious views and values, as well as resistance and reaction.

The extension of civic rights in Western Europe and the growth of economic opportunity there, coupled with continued oppression in the Russian Empire, led to a migration westward. Most crossed the Atlantic to the New World and its promise of even greater freedom and opportunity.

Emancipation, enlightenment, and migration made the soil fertile for the sprouting and growth of Reform Judaism. Reform in turn brought about the organized opposition of the traditionalists, which made for a consciousness of their own corporate identity as Orthodox. The excesses of Reform led to the turning away of a leading participant, Zechariah Frankel, and his formulation of "positive historical Judaism," the forerunner of American Conservative Judaism. A traditionalist accommodation to the challenges of emancipation and enlightenment was Samson Raphael Hirsch's neo-Orthodoxy, which has been a major influence on modern American Orthodoxy.

The American counterpart experiences to the European emancipation, enlightenment, and migration were freedom, frontier, and immigration.

The Jesuit scholar Father Giovanni Antonio Grassi spent the years 1810–17 in America. His description of the religious scene is of significance to our considerations.

> By virtue of an article in the federal constitution every religion and every sect is fully tolerated, is equally protected, and equally treated in the United States. . . . Every sect there is held as good, every road is correct. . . .
>
> In accordance with such principles, it is not surprising if America gives birth to innumerable sects which daily subdivide and multiply.[1]

In the early 1830s Alexis de Tocqueville wrote:

> The sects which exist in the United States are innumerable. They all differ in respect to worship which is due from man to his Creator, but they all agree in respect to the duties which are due from man to man. . . . There is no country in the whole world in which the Christian religion retains a greater influence over the souls of men than in America. . . . The Americans combine the notions of Christianity and of liberty so intimately in their minds, that it is impossible to make them conceive the one without the other.[2]

Grassi, the priest, is struck by the proliferation of sects which freedom permits. The layman, Tocqueville, noting the same, understands that freedom which permits division on matters of doctrine, unites men in their esteem of religion as a necessary force in the service of democracy and liberty. In a word, democracy needs *religion*, freedom permits *religions*.

Throughout the nineteenth century, America was a moving frontier. On the frontier, the value of the church as a civilizing, culturizing, stabilizing force was understood and appreciated. At the same time, the free, often iconoclastic spirits who were drawn to the frontier, and the experimentation and innovation which took place in all manner of endeavors, made the frontier hospitable to proliferating sects and new statements in doctrine and forms of religion.

Early in the century, Moses Hart, scion of the leading pioneer Jewish family of Canada, residing in New York, attempted to fashion a new religion for America. He felt that the existing religions were strongly chequered with . . . dangerous and disrespectful principles, which ought to be plucked from the fair soil of America." In his *Modern Religion* he called to Americans

> your rapid progress in free principles and toleration, have drawn forth the smiles of applause from Europe, Asia, and Africa.
>
> One task remains, may you soon bury their religious superstition in the vast ocean which separates you from them. The author is humbly offering for your adoption a system of religion, styled Modern Religion.[3]

The New World demands a new religion!

In 1844 Daniel Rupp published his *An Original History of the Religious Denominations at Present Existing in the United States.* What is noteworthy is that the accounts were written "expressly for the work by eminent theological professors, ministers and lay members of the respective denominations." No less than forty-three denominations are represented. Baptist, Presbyterian, Protestant Episcopal; and Congregationalist leaders had no objection to having their denominations listed with the Mennonites, the Amish, the Millenarians, the Shakers, the Schwenkfelders, the Latter Day Saints, and the Jews. The listing is in alphabetical order. The length of the essays was determined, apparently, by the authors. There being no established church, each denomination felt the equal of any other.

Some forty million immigrants came to America during the century. They brought with them their religious ways, and established institutions to serve and perpetuate them. Immigration itself made for the proliferation of sects.

The professional Jewish traveler I. J. Benjamin II visited America in 1859–62. He lists twenty-three congregations in New York City.

In each instance he notes the ritual or ethnic composition of the congregation, e.g., "Polish ritual," "This is a Dutch congregation," "Bohemian ritual," "German ritual," "organized in 1859 by French Jews," etc.[4]

Initially attempts were made to fashion an American Judaism.

"The massacre of Damascus," Mordecai Manuel Noah wrote to Isaac Leeser, "was considered a terrible infliction—terrible it was no doubt to the sufferers—but I have always deemed it a most providential dispensation. . . . the governments of the earth loudly denounced the cruelties practiced toward Jews." Jewish communities the world over were shocked and aroused, and those who dared organize and speak protest did so. The news from Syria in 1840 galvanized the Jews of America into action. The Jews of New York, Philadelphia, Cincinnati, and Richmond united in individual communal expressions of horror, sympathy, and indignation. Participation in a common cause which so excited the emotions brought the disparate elements of the American Jewish community together. The American Jewish community had its beginnings as a self-conscious entity in the activity precipitated by "the massacre of Damascus."

A number of Philadelphians led by the Reverend Isaac Leeser, distressed with the anarchy which marked Jewish life in 1840 America, but heartened by the example of Jews of different congregations uniting for common effort, decided to attempt a Union of American Israelites. If the Jews of America could unite to protect their brother's body, would they not join together for the enhancement of their children's souls?

In July 1841 a circular was sent to the congregations of the United States. "The Israelites of Philadelphia" sent "greetings" and invited fellow American Jews.

> In the full confidence that you will favorably entertain our plan for a general union, we, on the part of the Israelites of this vicinity, affectionately invite you to deliberate well on the proposition and regulations which accompany this, and to elect without delay suitable persons for delegates, to meet us in general convention, on the first Sunday in November, being the 7th of the month, corresponding with the 23rd day of Mar-cheshvan, 5602, at Philadelphia.[5]

The accompanying "proposition and regulations" detailed plans for a national religious authority, a system of elementary and higher Jewish education, and a union of American Jewish congregations.

Later, Leeser ruefully reminisced:

> The circular, with the preliminary adopted constitution, was sent to the few congregations then existing in the country; but, in brief, the conference did not meet; no rabbinical authority was instituted, no school was erected, no union was established, and the incipient division and strife were permitted to take what shape they pleased.[6]

A second attempt to forge an American Israel was through a conference which met in Cleveland, Ohio, in October 1855. It sought to unite the traditionalist and liberal forces. For the sake of Jewish religious unity, the leaders of the respective groups, Isaac Leeser and Isaac Mayer Wise, put aside differences which had led to animosity. Leeser's contribution was in his attendance, thus giving recognition to rabbis of the Reform school. Wise's offering on the altar of unity was ideological. He accepted the proposition: "The Talmud contains the traditional, legal and logical exposition of the biblical laws which must be expounded and practiced according to the comments of the Talmud."[7]

The conference and its principles drew opposition from the Right and from the Left. Rabbi David Einhorn and members of his Har Sinai Congregation of Baltimore published a protest, declaring that "The said platform would condemn Judaism to a perpetual stagnation."

Isaac Leeser, after initial exultation of what he considered a triumph for traditionalism, took a second look and did not like what he saw. Wise's acceptance of the statement on talmudic law was not, as Leeser first hailed it, "a son of Israel has repentantly revoked the rebellion he had uttered," but a strategic move to establish a united American Israel to which he, Wise, would give leadership.

The Cleveland Conference did not heal the breach between reformers and traditionalists. It led to further division, causing a breach within Reform itself: the practical moderate Reform of Isaac Mayer Wise and the ideological radical Reform of David Einhorn.

A threefold division in American Jewish religious life was noted in 1871 by W. M. Rosenblatt. In an article in the *Galaxy*, he divides American Jewry into Orthodox, Conservative, and Radical.[8] Wise and Company are the conservatives; the Einhorn group, the radicals.

The divisions in American Jewry were pronounced, the polemics sharp, and the controversies continuous. The pages of the contemporary Jewish press, the *Occident*, the *Israelite*, *Sinai*, the *Asmonean*, are replete with attack and counterattack, accusation and counter-accusation. And small wonder. Religious controversy, the sharpest polemics and the vilest accusations were part of the nineteenth-century American religious scene. Religious controversy was rife in European Jewry. American Jewry, being part of both, responded and participated. Controversies are exciting and polemics stimulating, but they placed a struggling new enterprise in mortal peril. American Judaism was not so firmly established as to afford itself the luxury of division and diversity.

The death of Isaac Leeser in 1867 left the traditionalist forces without an effective leader or spokesman. The field was open wide for the spread of Reform, and spread it did. Virtually all the leading congregations soon were in the Reform fold, and almost all the leading rabbinical personalities were in its camp. An attempt was made in 1869 to unite Reform Jewry, the first step of which was a rabbinic conference held in Philadelphia.

The convener of the conference and its leading spirit was David Einhorn. Isaac Mayer Wise was in attendance. The Seven Resolutions adopted pronounced Einhorn's ideology. The emphasis is on the denial of Jewish nationality and separateness. Diaspora is not punishment but divinely ordained opportunity for the Jews to fulfill "their high priestly task to lead the nations in the true knowledge and worship of God." The one "practical" plank declared that because Hebrew has become "incomprehensible for the overwhelming majority of our present-day co-religionists . . . in the act of prayer Hebrew must take second place behind a language which the worshippers can understand."

A quarter of a century earlier, Zechariah Frankel had left the Frankfort Conference and Reform Judaism on the issue of the place of Hebrew in worship. Wise was not ready to go that far, but he must have bridled at this anti-Hebrew plank. Only a year earlier, in his introduction to his *Hymns, Psalms and Prayers,* he had written:

> The Hebrew language in our public worship is the medium of our synagogal union. Dispersed as the house of Israel is in all lands, we must have a vehicle to understand each other in the house of God, so that no brother be a stranger therein; and this vehicle is the Hebrew.

He returned to Cincinnati sobered and humbled. He recognized radical Reform as a divisive rather than uniting force. His essential commitment was not to Reform Judaism but to an American Judaism. At the conference he was a participant, not a leader. Though he continued formal participation with the rabbinic body which had met in Philadelphia, he knew that this was not a vehicle for the fashioning of an American Judaism.

The Eastern Seaboard was dominated by the proponents of radical Reform. Wise's influence was strong in the West and South. Gifted organizer that he was, he understood that congregations could be united through participation in a project rather than through agreement on resolutions. A "Jewish Theological Institute" to educate an American Jewish ministry was the vehicle. To establish and maintain such an institution, a call was issued by the congregations of Cincinnati

> to all congregations of the West and South for a Congregational Convention to form a "Union of Congregations" under whose auspices a "Jewish Theological Institute" shall be established, and other measures adopted which will advance the prosperity of our religion.[10]

Note, it is an appeal to *all* congregations. No mention of reform. It is to "advance the prosperity of our religion." It was to be a "Union of American Hebrew Congregations" of all views and all hues.

The union prospered; the college was launched and maintained. Wise was able to attract to the enterprise even so staunch a traditionalist as Sabato Morais, hazzan minister of the Mikveh Israel Congregation, Philadelphia. Morais addressed the fourth annual session of the council in 1877 and served on the examining committee, signing a report which read in part:

The College in Cincinnati may unequivocally be pronounced an object deserving the support of all Israelites who wish that attachment to the ancestral faith be founded upon a knowledge of its precepts, and an extensive acquaintance with the national literature.[11]

In 1880 the dream of a united American Jewish religious community seemed not only attainable but well on the road to fulfillment. There was little strength or vitality in Orthodoxy and no hope for its future. Einhorn's death in 1879 left a void of leadership in the radical forces. Wise's union and college were prospering and attracting an ever larger and ever more diversified affiliation and support.

The Decisive Decade

The bomb which took the life of Alexander II, "Czar of all the Russians," in March 1881, ushered in a new era in American Jewish life. Until then Jewish immigration to America had been steady but moderate, and largely from Western and Central Europe. The pogroms and restrictive "May Laws" of 1882 touched off a mass migration of East European Jews.

In the decade 1880–90, some 200,000 East European Jews came to America, doubling the Jewish population. In the next decade the number doubled again. A new community was in the making, of a different ethnic composition and having new religious views and needs.

Three events took place in the middle of the ninth decade of the nineteenth century which concretized the division of the American Jewish religious community into the present groupings of Orthodox, Conservative, and Reform.

In 1885 nineteen leading Reform rabbis met in Pittsburgh and adopted a declaration of principles which remained the operative though unofficial platform of Reform Judaism for more than half a century. A year later a group of scholarly rabbis and traditionally oriented laymen founded the Jewish Theological Seminary of America. Two years after that the Orthodox congregations of New York brought to these shores Rabbi Jacob Joseph to serve as their chief rabbi.

The platform adopted in Pittsburgh adopted principles, eight in number, which were of such a radical nature that they brought forth immediate criticism and denunciation, and roused those who were critical to concrete counter-action. Sabato Morais stated that "the platform reveals an unwarrantable antagonism to the five holy books." His fellow Sephardi minister, H. Pereira Mendes, declared: "They may give up . . . the doctrine of a restoration in Palestine if they like. But I prefer Isaiah, Jeremiah, Ezekiel. . . . Forgive me again, if I prefer His voice to the voices of these ministers." The action they jointly undertook was to found a seminary.

The establishment of the Jewish Theological Seminary of America, in 1886, laid the foundation for what was later to become the Conservative movement. The immediate motivations for the founding of the seminary were negative rather than positive. Like many religious movements, Conservative Judaism had its beginnings in protest. In 1884, at the banquet held in celebration of the first graduation from the Hebrew Union College (then the only rabbinical seminary in America), the food served was not kosher. Suspicions about the college which had been smoldering for some time now burst into open flame, and the traditional elements in American Jewry began to think of establishing an Orthodox theological seminary. A year later, the tone of the Pittsburgh Platform aroused the misgivings and opposition of a group of moderate Reform rabbis, who had long suspected that American Reform had permitted itself excesses which were as dangerous as they were drastic. The "dinner" and the "platform" brought together two forces which now found common ground in their opposition. They united in protest against the Hebrew Union College and the Pittsburgh Conference, and gave constructive expression to their disapproval through the founding of a seminary which would chart a new course for American Israel.

The antecedents for the Conservative tendency institutionalized in the seminary were twofold. Sabato Morais, the seminary's first president, was the minister of Mikve Israel, the Sephardi congregation of Philadelphia. Another of the seminary's founders, H. Pereira Mendes, was the spiritual head of Shearith Israel, the Spanish and Portuguese Synagogue in New York. Their co-worker, Bernard

Drachman, was rabbi of an Orthodox congregation in New York, of the West European mode. All three were Orthodox. Co-founders Alexander Kohut, Marcus Jastrow, and Benjamin Szold were rabbis of moderate Reform congregations, and ideologically committed to the "positive historical" view of Judaism of Zechariah Frankel, principal of the Jewish Theological Seminary of Breslau.

"Positive historical Judaism," as formulated by Frankel and his disciples, and which became the cornerstone for the growing edifice of Conservative ideology, viewed Judaism as the product of historical development. It called for a positive attitude of reverence and understanding toward traditional Judaism. The complex of values, practices, and ideals of traditional Judaism was not to be lightly surrendered for the sake of convenience, conformity, or material advantage. The specifically Jewish elements in Judaism, as, for example, the Hebrew language, were considered essential to the preservation of its character and vitality.

Conservative Judaism was a "threefold cord" whose strands were the scientific study of Judaism of the "positive historical" school, the congregational manner and mode of Sephardi and West European synagogues, and the piety and zeal of East European Orthodoxy.

From the beginning, the leaders of the seminary looked to the dramatically emerging East European Jewish community in America as a source of students and of congregations for its graduates. But the East European Orthodox community did not respond with support for the seminary. It had a plan and project of its own: to organize itself into an Association of the American Hebrew Congregations and bring a chief rabbi to these shores. *A Call*, issued April 1888, tells the purpose, the project, and the hope:

> in this land, where we are at liberty to observe our religion, to study, teach, observe, perform and establish our Law, we find that our religion is neglected and our Law held in light esteem. . . . Rouse yourselves and let not the mistake be repeated and continued by which Orthodox Judaism has lost so many who should be enlisted under its banner. Certain congregations have united in order to create an intelligent orthodoxy, and to prove that also in America can be combined honor, enlightenment and culture, with a proper observance of religious duty.

> After much care in the choice of a Chief Rabbi, we have selected the
> learned and pious Rabbi Jacob Joseph of Vilna. He is to be the leader in
> the battle which must be waged to keep the next generation faithful to
> Judaism in spite of educational, social and business influences which, in
> America, are so powerful to make our sons and daughters forget their
> duty to the religion in which their ancestors lived, and for which those
> ancestors died.

The rabbi was greeted with all hope and enthusiasm. The press
was full of his doings. But after a brief flush of success, the whole
endeavor disintegrated into a debacle and worse. I have written the
full story elsewhere.[12] But the attempt had its lasting effect and value
as well. It introduced the East European Jew into communal
activities and religious organization on these shores. The organization of the association and the enthusiasm it evoked demonstrated
the latent vitality of Orthodoxy. The vitality evidenced no doubt
encouraged the establishment of the Union of Orthodox Jewish
Congregations of America a decade later. In any case, Orthodoxy
had now declared and established itself as an independent,
self-conscious religious movement. After these events there was no
turning back.

Each movement's project was appropriate to its philosophy of
Judaism and in answer to its immediate and future needs.

Reform had been largely rejection; a statement of affirmation was
needed. Because each rabbi felt free to act as he saw fit and to espouse
what he alone felt right, the movement was fragmented. It needed
agreement on basic principles and cohesion in views and ways. A
declaration of principles, a commonly accepted platform, was the
need and at Pittsburgh became the reality.

Conservative Judaism, at the same time faithful to traditional
ways and open to development and change, needed a clergy expert in
the tradition yet part of the contemporary scene. A seminary was
therefore established to train American young men in the tradition,
which they would then expound in contemporaneous, meaningful
fashion and adapt to the spiritual needs of their congregants.

For Orthodoxy the truth of word and deed was in the Tradition as
received and transmitted. What was needed was an authority to

expound it, apply it, enforce it—a rabbi respected for his scholarship and therefore accepted as *the* authority.

By 1890 the pattern was set for American Judaism. Reform was armed with an ideology. Conservative Judaism had its struggling ·seminary and the hope that its graduates would fashion a "way" for American Israel. Orthodoxy, having flexed its organizational muscles, felt ready for and looked to an ever-increasing immigration to bring it adherents and the strength they would provide.

The Synagogue in America

On March 18, 1655, Domine Johannes Megapolensis of the Dutch Reformed Church of New Amsterdam wrote his superiors in Amsterdam:

> Last summer some Jews came here from Holland in order to trade. Afterwards, some Jews, poor and healthy, also came here on the same ship with Domine Polheijmius. . . . Now again, in the spring some have come from Holland, and report that a great many of that lot would yet follow and then build here their synagogue.[13]

The domine feared that the immigrant Jews would establish a congregation and build a synagogue. That this was their desire and request is borne out by a letter sent by Governor Peter Stuyvesant to the directors of the Dutch West India Company, June 10, 1656:

> . . . . they (the Jewish nation) have many times requested of us the free and public exercise of their abominable religion, but this cannot yet be accorded them. What they may be able to obtain from your honors time will tell.[14]

The Jews of New Amsterdam, helped by their co-religionists in Amsterdam, must have continued to press their demands, for Stuyvesant has again to plea to his superiors not to grant them the right of public worship: "To give liberty to the Jews will be very detrimental here. . . . giving them liberty, we cannot refuse the Lutherans and Papists."[15]

The Shearith Israel Congregation, mother synagogue of American Israel, may very well be right in dating its inception to 1654. On

February 2, 1656, in reply to a petition of the Jews of the settlement for consent to "purchase a burying place," it was voted "to point out to the petitioners a little hook of land situated outside of this city for a burial place."[16] The first congregation's initial holding, as was the case with many of its daughter congregations, was a cemetery. Worship could be held in any place or building. What was required was a *minyan*, the quorum of worshippers, not a synagogue. Burial, however, demanded consecrated ground. For the Shearith Israel Congregation, the synagogue followed the cemetery after six and a half decades. But a congregation it was, serving the spiritual, cultural, and social needs of its people.

In colonial America, congregation and community were synonymous, and the congregation served all communal needs. In European countries the Jew was a member of the Jewish community. He became so through birth, and the law of the land considered him as such unless he willingly dissociated himself from it through conversion to another faith. In America, one was born into citizenship and became a member of a religious group through an act of association or affiliation. For the American Jew, congregation replaced community as the vehicle for Jewish association and identification.

The American Synagogue

Six synagogues served colonial Jewry in New York, Newport, Philadelphia, Richmond, Charleston, and Savannah. All used the Sefardi ritual though the majority of the congregants were Ashkenazi. Thus the draft of a constitution for Philadelphia's Mikveh Israel Congregation was written in Yiddish, but the synagogue ritual was Sefardi. The language was Yiddish because the congregants were German immigrants. Similarly, the Ashkenazim outnumbered the Sephardim in New York's Shearith Israel by 1710, but its rite remained, as it does to the present day, Sephardi. I would conjecture that this anomaly was due to the fact that the immigrant considered the rite not so much Sephardi as American. The synagogue he found was not only an institution of Jewish life, it was also a component of the American religious landscape, standing side by side with the churches of the community.

It was not only the Jew but his neighbors as well who looked upon the synagogue as an American institution and as a symbol of liberty and equality. Thus the *Savannah Republican* of April 21, 1820, reports:

> On Wednesday the Grand Lodge of Georgia, and subordinate Lodges of this city, assembled . . . for the purpose of . . . laying . . . the cornerstone of a Hebrew synagogue.

Thomas P. Charlton, grand master of the Masons of Georgia and mayor of Savannah, stated in his address:

> This ceremony is a beautiful illustration of our happy, tolerant, and free government. . . . where is this persuasion more respected and better protected?

The newspaper report comments:

> It was highly gratifying to the sincere friends of our glorious constitution, to see a sect, believing so implicitly in that Almighty whom WE ALL adore—suffered to enjoy the privileges of American citizens, and to worship, in their own Temple, in the manner of their forefathers.[17]

The American Jew established congregations and built synagogues not only in answer to his own spiritual needs, but also as his contribution to American religious life and as a symbol of his participation in the blessings of liberty which America extended. For those who had seen synagogues at best tolerated in the lands of their birth, the freedom to worship and the encouragement to build which they found in America became a mandate. Small wonder, then, that congregations were established whenever the requisite quorum was obtained and that synagogues were built as soon as ability matched desire.

A Jewish Calendar, published in 1854, contains a listing of Jewish congregations in America. It is noteworthy that in the state of California, in 1853, there existed congregations in:

> Columma on the Yuba River, organized 1850.
> Maryville, Temporary Synagogue and Hebrew Benevolent Society.

Nevada City, the number of Israelites in the city in 5613 (1853) was thirty.
Sacramento
San Diego
San Francisco (three congregations and two benevolent societies)
Sonora
Stockton, which also had a *Society of Lovely Nation* for attendance on the sick and the dead.[18]

In his *Culture on the Moving Frontier*, Louis B. Wright states: "Of all the agencies utilized by man in maintaining traditional civilization on the successive frontiers in America, it should now be abundantly clear that none was more effective than organized religion."[19]

Religion was not only a civilizing force, but a stabilizing, culturizing, and socializing force as well. The church was esteemed on the frontier for performing these needed functions. Churches were established to perform them, and synagogues as well.

The Synagogue in the Mid-Nineteenth Century

The community-congregations of early America began to give way to *minhag* congregations, i.e., synagogues organized by individuals coming from the same land or area, accustomed to worship in a particular rite. Thus I. J. Benjamin II, in listing the congregations of New York, states their *minhag*, or synagogal rite, Polish or German. Rodef Sholom of Philadelphia was organized by German Jews who did not want to worship in the Sephardi rite, and a group who felt similarly left Shearith Israel to form B'nai Jeshurun in New York City in 1825.

Congregations also began to be founded as ideological expressions. Thus, when the petition of forty-seven members of Beth Elohim of Charleston, South Carolina, was rejected by the adjunta, they formed the Reformed Society of Israelites in 1825. It lasted less than a decade, but it prepared the way for the establishment of Reform congregations. The first was the Har Sinai Verein in Baltimore, organized in 1842 by a group of German immigrants influenced by the Hamburg (Germany) Temple Movement. They held services of Rosh Hashanah of that year using the Hamburg prayer book, singing hymns from the Hamburg hymn book to the accompaniment of a parlor organ.

The congregational history of Temple Emanuel in New York, published in celebration of its Jubilee in 1895, tells of its founding:

> The Congregation of Emanu-El is a child of German origin, and was nourished and raised at the fountain-well of Jewish theological science, according to German interpretation.
>
> In the fourth decade of the present century there came to this country a number of Israelites from Germany, who seem to have been drawn together here by the liberal views which they held concerning religious affairs. . . . They formed a society which they called the "Cultus Verein," or Culture Society. On the 6th day of April, 1845, when their society had thirty-three members, they called a general meeting, at which a resolution was passed, organizing themselves into a regular Congregation under the name of Emanu-El (God with us).[20]

In the sixties and seventies most congregations began to institute reforms, moderate and radical as well. Thus, for example, the Berith Kodesh Congregation of Rochester, New York, introduced the organ and choir music into its services in 1862. Family pews were introduced in 1869. This led to a division within the congregation and the resignation of a group which founded a new, more traditional congregation.

A year after the pews incident, some of the more radical members succeeded in bringing the Reverend N. Mann, pastor of the Unitarian Society, to the temple to lecture. A large assemblage of Jews and non-Jews was present to witness this innovation. In 1873 a Union Thanksgiving Service was instituted in which Jewish and Unitarian congregations joined for worship.

In 1879 David Rosenberg was elected president on the promise that he would remove his hat at services when occupying his official seat. He did so, bringing "down upon his unprotected head a storm of indignation and abuse from the older members." Nevertheless, during his administration the rule was passed that abolished hat-wearing in the temple. In 1883 the temple introduced a new ritual almost entirely in English. "It was believed to be the first temple in the United States, and probably in the world, to take this step."

While the great majority of American synagogues were turning to Reform, a new kind of congregation was being introduced to the American scene, the East European Orthodox synagogue.

A typical congregation was Beth Israel of Rochester. Its history discloses a determined effort to insulate itself against the influences of the American environment. The world about was the enemy, and the synagogue had to be kept apart and separate as a refuge and sanctuary from the spiritually corroding forces in the economic, social, and cultural life of the immigrant community. The men of Beth Israel through their isolation were not ignoring the America they knew, but reacting to it and against it, even as the architects of Reform for Berit Kodesh were accommodating and yielding to it. For the immigrant Jew viewed America as a melting pot.

The melting-pot concept of America proclaimed: America welcomes all peoples, all nationalities. It extends to them the privileges of political freedom and the promise of economic opportunity. In turn it asks that peoples and nationalities cast off their folkways, their traditions, whatever made them distinct and distinguished. In turn they were to adopt the way of life which was emerging from the fusing fires of the great melting pot—America. This was the price one had to pay for the prize of being an American. Most thought the prize well worth the price.

Within the Jewish community there ensued a mighty endeavor to accommodate the Jew to America, the melting pot. America was looked upon as a monolith, a jealous god admitting of no diversity in loyalty. In return America offered you not merely acceptance as an American, but your fusing into America and your becoming an integral part of it.

How could the immigrant or second-generation Jew resist its appeal?

Rabbi Charles Fleischer of Boston's Temple Israel urged Jews to intermarry to build the "new nation . . . to emerge from the melting pot." And he continued to serve the temple as its spiritual leader.

The strong assimilationist program and practices of radical Reform were in response to America, the melting pot. The early history of East European Orthodoxy in the United States, its withdrawal and self-imposed spiritual ghettoization, was in reaction to such an America. This jealous crucible admitted of no middle ground. You surrendered or you withdrew, and the Jewish religious community became two communities as a result. The American synagogue was turned into a churchlike temple in the one, and an insulated shtibl in the other.

Beyond the Melting Pot

In the second decade of the twentieth century there was a new look at the melting pot. The product which comes out of the melting pot is a dull, drab, lacklustre metal. Was this to be America? Was it to the benefit of America to cast in the cauldron the glittering gold, the shimmering silver, the supple copper, even the hard-stoked iron of national characteristics and ethnic distinctiveness and thus remove from the landscape of America these precious metals—precious because their uniqueness and distinctiveness gave color and glow to America? The lilting song which was America was in danger of becoming a monotonous hum.

Horace Kallen sounded the alarm and proposed a solution. "Democracy Versus the Melting Pot" he called his pronouncement, which appeared in the *Nation* in 1915. His was a new image of America.

> Its form is that of the Federal republic: its substance a democracy of nationalities, co-operating voluntarily and autonomously in the enterprise of self-realization through the perfection of men according to their kind. . . . As in an orchestra, every type of instrument has its specific timbre and tonality, founded in its substance and form; as every type has its appropriate theme and melody in the whole symphony, so in society each ethnic group is the natural instrument, its spirit and culture are its theme and melody, and the harmony and dissonances and discords of them all make the symphony of civilization.[21]

America would be best served, its people would find greatest fulfillment, through cultural pluralism.

This new image of America was seized upon as a "democratic

imperative" by individuals and groups of men committed to Jewish survival and Jewish cultural creativity. Mordecai M. Kaplan gave it philosophical exposition in terms of modern Jewish experience and needs.

The synagogue reacted by transforming itself from a house of prayer to a synagogue center with a program designed "to meet the spiritual, cultural and social needs of every member of every family."

Reports of congregational life and activities in the early 1920s describe its program. In a large city:

> *Congregation B'nai Jeshurun, Cleveland, Ohio:*
> Very few congregations in this country have the large and varied number of activities of Congregation B'nai Jeshurun. Among them are:
> THE AIN JACOB GROUP of middle-aged men who meet on Sabbath afternoons and are led by Rabbi Solomon Goldman.
> THE SHABBOS TEA attracts from three to five hundred women each fortnight.
> THE SCHOOL FOR ADULTS meeting every Monday night for two hours . . . eighty students.
> YOUNG WOMEN'S LITERARY UNIT . . .
> ALUMNI DRAMATIC CLUB . . . arranges readings and presentations for the Shabbos teas.
> HIGH SCHOOL DEPARTMENT . . . The faculty are all college graduates . . . An annual called "Jeshurunite" . . . 25 graduates . . . enrollment of 150.
> THE SCHOOL . . . Hebrew School meets first four days of week . . . five year curriculum . . . faculty of seven . . . 300 students . . . Religious School . . . Sundays . . . 27 teachers . . . enrollment of 560.
> THE WOMEN'S BIBLE CLASS. . . Tuesday afternoon for study of Bible. . . enrollment of 20.
> JUNIOR CLUBS. . . Literary and dramatic.
> SATURDAY NIGHTERS. . . Young men and women. . . college graduates. . . papers prepared by members of group. . . This group is the "talk of the town" and the privilege of membership—or even visiting privilege—is eagerly sought.

And in a small town:

BLUEFIELD, WEST VIRGINIA

What can be done in a small community can be learned to advantage from the survey of what is being done in Bluefield, W. Virginia. There, through the activities of the ladies, the congregation succeeded in getting practically a one hundred percent attendance at all services, and the attendance of almost every Jewish child at religious school. The holidays are celebrated by every member of the town with a fine communal spirit. On Shabuot, for instance, the children will take a prominent part. The young people who comprise the Progress Club will stage a sketch entitled "Shabuot.". . . The Bluefield chapter of the Hadassah will act as hostesses of the evening, and the congregation will present every boy and girl with a Biblical history.

In the Post War World

The historian Marcus L. Hansen proposed the thesis: "What the son wishes to forget, the grandson wishes to remember." C. Bezalel Sherman points out that

> Alone of all the white ethnic groups do American Jews supply proof for the correctness of the Hansen thesis. Only among them do the grandchildren manifest a greater desire to be part of the community than the children of immigrants.[22]

"The third generation of American Jews," writes Will Herberg, "instead of somehow finally getting rid of their Jewishness, as the Italians were getting rid of their 'Italianness' and the Poles of their 'Polishness' actually began to *reassert* their Jewish identification and to *return* to their Jewishness." He offers the explanation:

> The young Jew for whom the Jewish immigrant-ethnic group had lost all meaning because he was an American and not a foreigner, could still think of himself as a Jew, because to him being a Jew now meant identification with the Jewish religious community.[23]

The third-generation Jew returned not to the mores and folkways of his immigrant grandparents, but to the faith of his forefathers. The American Jew began to react to a new image of America: America as a land of "ethnic assimilation and religious differentiation." "The Land of the Three Great Faiths," Herberg termed it.

America as a nation demands political unity and civic concern, but it also fosters religious diversity. The Jew, sensing this, has made synagogue affiliation his expression of Jewish association. He has quickly learned that the community in which he lives not only looks upon him as a member of a religious group, but expects of him at least nominal association with the institution of the Jewish religious community—the synagogue.

Because of this, in Marshall Sklare's words: "The institutional growth of the synagogue movement since World War II has been exceedingly impressive."

This was not merely a post–World War II phenomenon; it had its roots in earlier Jewish experience. Salo Baron, in a discussion entitled "Religion or Ethnic Community?", pointed out:

> In western Europe and America, the religious factor has retained its pre-eminent position in the scale of communal values. . . . the religious congregation has continued to attract the relatively most constant and active participation of a large membership. . . . [The work of the Jewish Federations of Charities] can never hope to attract the same intensity of allegiance or even the same extensity of effort as has so long been the case with the Synagogue. . . . total congregational member-ship in the United States vastly exceeds, numerically, Jewish membership in purely philanthropic undertakings.[24]

In post–World War II America, the Jew expressed his Jewish association through synagogue affiliation. The congregation be-came, in scope and function, a miniature community, striving to provide for the spiritual, cultural, and social needs of the congregants. The congregational school became the preeminent Jewish educational institution. Lectures, classes, programs of music and art were provided for the adults. The men's club and sisterhood undertood to furnish fellowship and activity.

The synagogue fashioned in the era of cultural pluralism was expanded in program and activities, and occupied a place of centrality in the life of the community and the individual Jew. Whether pious or not, the American Jew accepted the image of religious community and its institutionalization in the synagogue as right and desirable.

And Now . . .

In his *The Rise of the Unmeltable Ethnics*, Michael Novak calls the 1970s the "Decade of the Ethnic." The United States Department of Health, Education and Welfare, the *New York Times* reported on October 5, 1974, has launched a campaign of public-service television spots which "concentrate on the problems and value of an ethnically mixed society . . ." Impressive evidence can be marshaled to document the observation that Americans are opting for ethnic identity. "Black is beautiful," "Kiss me, I'm Irish," "Sound the horn if you're Italian," are the most visible manifestations, but the turn from religious identity to ethnic goes deeper than bumper-sticker slogans. We might then expect a crisis confronting the religious establishment, and data pointing to diminishing affiliation and support of churches would indicate that this has indeed happened. National church bodies have slashed their staffs and budgets. Protestant and Catholic theological seminaries are consolidating or closing.

Once again the Jewish community seems to be an exception. There is little evidence that Jews are anxious to call themselves a religious minority. Synagogues have retained their membership to a remarkable degree. The student bodies of the Jewish seminaries have increased in number, and a new seminary, the Reconstructionist, has come into being.

There is every reason to believe that into the foreseeable future the synagogue will continue to maintain its centrality in Jewish life. It seems equally clear that the other striking feature of American Jewish religious life, its tripartite denominationalism, will continue.

The historical experience of the Jew in America has indicated to him that the synagogue, alert to the American realities and responsive to changing Jewish needs, is the most viable and vital vehicle for the expression of his identity and the fostering of his spiritual and cultural interests.

We have thus seen the changing nature of the American synagogue. In colonial days, congregation and community were synonymous. The early republic saw the beginnings of the "rite congregation," and later the ideological division into the traditional synagogue, and the Reform temple. The melting pot image

produced the radical Reform temple and the insular Orthodox *shul.*
Cultural pluralism gave rise to the synagogue center. The imaging of
America as the Land of the Three Great Faiths gave the synagogue
centrality in Jewish life, and enabled it to expand its program and
activities to include the totality of spiritual, cultural and social life.

At all times, the synagogue responded to and provided for the felt
needs of the congregants—now immigrant, now engaged in
Americanization, now at home in America.

The American Jew is equally aware that as America is a pluralistic
society, so the American Jewish community will be characterized by
a diversity in unity (even as it is strengthened by a basic unity in that
diversity). Its pluralistic character is, and will continue to be,
expressed by the tripartite religious grouping, Orthodox-
Conservative-Reform.

The American Jew lives, then, in a dual pluralism, that of
America and that of his own community.

Professor Winthrop S. Hudson, in his *Religion in America,* writes:

> Perhaps one of the greatest contributions of Judaism to the United
> States will be to help other Americans understand how the United
> States can be a truly pluralistic society in which the pluralism is
> maintained in a way that is enriching rather than impoverishing . . .[25]

The challenge before the religiously pluralistic American Jewish
community is to guard against the diversity becoming mean and
divisive, communally disruptive and spiritually impoverishing. It
can become culturally creative and religiously enriching if (I apply
the observation of Professor Hudson to this context) "the integrity of
the different faiths is preserved while adherents of the several
traditions engage in open dialogue that will clarify and deepen their
own self-understanding."

If this can be done, then American Jewry can, with all seriousness,
accept the observation and challenge of Professor Hudson as an
opportunity for high and signal service to America.

> Perhaps one of the greatest contributions of Judaism to the United
> States will be to help other Americans understand how the United

States can be a truly pluralistic society . . . a society of dual
commitments which need not be in conflict but can be complementary.
From the long experience of Judaism, Americans of other faiths can
learn how this may be done with both grace and integrity.[26]

NOTES

1. *This Was America*, ed. Oscar Handlin (Harper Torchbooks, 1949), pp. 147–50.
2. Alexis de Tocqueville, *Democracy in America* (New York: Colonial Press, 1899), vol. 1, pp. 308, 311.
3. M. Hart, *Modern Religion* (New York 1824), p. 11.
4. *Three Years in America* (Jewish Publication Society, 1956), vol. 1, pp. 50 ff.
5. *Circular, Philadelphia, Ab 5601, July, 1841.*
6. *Occident* 17, no. 14 (June 30, 1859): 80.
7. Gunther Plaut, *The Growth of Reform Judaism* (New York, 1965), p. 20.
8. New York, January 1872, vol. 13, no. 1, pp. 47 ff.
9. Isaac M. Wise et al. *Hymns, Psalms and Prayers* (Cincinnati, 1868).
10. *Proceedings of the Union of American Hebrew Congregations* 1 (1879): 4.
11. Ibid., p. 524.
12. "New York Chooses a Chief Rabbi," *Publications of the American Jewish Historical Society* 44, no. 3 (March 1955).
13. *Ecclesiastical Records of New York*, I, 335.
14. Samuel Oppenheim, *Publications of American Jewish Historical Society*, vol. 18, p. 22.
15. Ibid., pp. 19, 20.
16. Ibid., p. 75.
17. *Savannah Republican*, April 21, 1820, p. 2.
18. Jacques J. Lyons and Abraham De Sola, *A Jewish Calendar for Fifty Years* (Montreal, 1854).
19. Louis B. Wright, *Culture on the Moving Frontier* (New York: Harper & Row, 1961), p. 168.
20. Myer, Stern, *The Rise and Progress of Reform Judaism* (New York, 1895).
21. Horace Kallen, *Culture and Democracy in the United States*, (New York, 1924), pp. 124–25.
22. C. Bezalel Sherman, *The Jew in American Society* (Detroit, 1961), p. 208.
23. Will Herberg, *Protestant-Catholic-Jew* (New York, 1955), pp. 201–2.
24. Salo Baron, *The Jewish Community* (Philadelphia, 1945), vol. 1, pp. 4–5.
25. Winthrop S. Hudson, *Religion in America*, 2d ed. (New York: Scribner's, 1973), p. 440.
26. Ibid., p. 441.

SELECTED BIBLIOGRAPHY

Davis, Moshe. *The Emergence of Conservative Judaism*. Philadelphia: Jewish Publication Society, 1963.
Glazer, Nathan. *American Judaism*. Chicago: University of Chicago Press, 1965.
Herberg, Will. *Protestant-Catholic-Jew*. New York: Doubleday & Co., Anchor Books, 1960.
Hudson, Winthrop S. *Religion in America*. 2d ed. New York: Scribner's, 1973.
Karp, Abraham J. *A History of the United Synagogue of America, 1913–1963*. New York: United Synagogue of America, 1964.

————. *New York Chooses a Chief Rabbi*. Waltham, Mass.: American Jewish Historical Society, 1955.

Korn, Bertram W., ed. *Retrospect and Prospect*. New York: Central Conference of American Rabbis, 1965.

Liebman, Charles S. "Orthodoxy in American Jewish Life." In *American Jewish Year Book*, vol. 66, Philadelphia: Jewish Publication Society, 1965.

Neusner, Jacob. *Understanding American Judaism*. 2 vols. New York: KTAV, 1975.

Parzen, Herbert. *Architects of Conservative Judaism*. New York: Jonathan David, 1964.

Plaut, W. Gunther. *The Growth of Reform Judaism*. New York: World Union for Progressive Judaism, 1965.

Sherman, C. Bezalel. *The Jew Within American Society*. Detroit: Wayne State University Press, 1965.

The Jewish Tradition in American Literature

DAVID MIRSKY

A DISCUSSION of American Jewish literature presupposes the existence of such a literature. It is only because there have been so deeply divergent, often intensely argued views on the matter that such a truism has to be put down. Through American Jewish writers, in the view of the distinguished British critic Walter Allen, "a recognizably new note has come into American fiction, not the less American for being unmistakably Jewish." Others, like Robert Alter, argue that only works written by Jews in a Jewish language, or which deal with distinctively Jewish subjects or draw upon recognizably Jewish literary traditions, can be properly referred to as Jewish literature, and Cynthia Ozick pleads for the development of a "new Yiddish" to permit American Jewish writers to produce American Jewish literature. Harry T. Moore points out "that some Jewish writers don't want to be thought of as Jewish writers, but as American writers," and he agrees with them. "Of course—and that is what they are," he states in a preface to Irving Mallin's book, *Jews and Americans*, which insists "that there is an American-Jewish context, *a 'community of feelings' which transcends individual style and different genres*."[1] The arguments go on, and this in itself should answer the question of what (or where, or why) is American Jewish writing. One may reject Bernard Sherman's contention "that Jewish-American literature is a distinct genre," but there are Jewish artists, recognizes *Medium*, "who are conscious of being Jews, of being heirs to a certain history and culture and of bringing that baggage with them to the esthetic enterprise."[2] Even Robert Alter grudgingly admits that "One cannot, however, simply discount the

79

possibility that some essentially Jewish qualities may adhere to the writing of the most thoroughly acculturated Jews."[3]

To identify some of these "essentially Jewish qualities," and to discover how they manifest themselves in American fiction, is the purpose of this paper.

Before proceeding to this task, let me briefly, probably imprudently, suggest a simple answer to a complex question: How does one account for the fact that, in Alvin Rosenfeld's words, "America's Jewish writers were the darlings of their literary generation, the new and major drive behind the renewal of American fiction in the decades immediately following World War Two"?[4]

The essence of the Jewish American historical experience has led to the blossoming of American Jewish letters. In America the Jew has been able to enter areas which in the past were closed to him. The process of wading into the mainstream of Western cultural life, which had begun in Europe during the nineteenth century, was a new and heady experience for the overwhelming majority of East European Jews who streamed to the United States at the end of the nineteenth and beginning of the twentieth centuries. They arrived, struggled to find roots, and finally established themselves firmly in the new land. The opportunity to move with comparative ease into all areas was exhilarating, even as it raised challenges and fears. Frenetically the Jew drove into all fields—commerce, politics, science, the professions, and also the arts—and faced a double challenge: finding success without losing traditional identity. This was not exclusively a Jewish experience; it was indeed a profoundly American one, but it was felt very keenly and poignantly by the Jew, more keenly and poignantly, perhaps, than by others, for two reasons. First, the Jew still had a fresh memory of his life in Eastern Europe, where he had been persecuted, restricted, denied the opportunity to venture beyond the confines of the *shtetel*. Second, even as the Golden Land allowed him to adventure with a hitherto unknown freedom, he could not help but be aware of the fact that his fellow Jews in other parts of the world still lived under the dark skies which he had escaped. This added intensity, as well as guilt, to his searches, and heightened awareness of his condition and the challenges he faced. The need to declare this awareness, to celebrate the new freedom, underscore its particularity, and adumbrate its challenges and threats, moved in many, and those who were appropriately gifted sought to express themselves through the arts, in themselves areas which in the past had been beyond their pale.

The Jewish tradition in the arts is rich, but for generations has been limited. Painting, for example, sculpture certainly, were not precincts Jews entered. A Jewish tradition of musical creativity did exist, limited, but not, as in the case of the visual and plastic arts, often proscribed. But a rich tradition in belles-lettres did exist, fed by reverence for the holy word, religious poetry, and sacred song. When he was kept outside the broader societal framework, the Jew restrained his artistic inclination or directed it elsewhere, but when the opportunity was offered, this inclination burgeoned richly. So it was in Moorish Spain, so it was in Renaissance Italy, so it was in twentieth-century America. In short, it was the exciting and energizing American experience which made it possible for the Jewish tradition to impress itself upon American letters.

Free to give full flight to his creative impulses, the Jewish writer sought to capture the fullness, the richness, and also the anxiety and the pain of life in America. He wrote as a Jew and drew upon the tradition and history which had shaped him, but he was giving expression to an American experience, an essential American experience. His work, therefore, spoke not only to Jews, but to non-Jews as well, and evoked a response in non-Jewish as well as Jewish America. Beginning with Abraham Cahan's *The Rise of David Levinsky*, the Jewish writer's move to eminence gained momentum between the two world wars, particularly during the thirties. It was only after World War II, however, after Hitler, the Holocaust, and Israel, as Fiedler declares,[5] that the Jewish writer assumed preeminence in American letters, allowing the tradition out of which he spoke to become a strong shaping force in American fiction.

In contemplating the Jewish tradition in American literature, I am struck by two phenomena which I believe make American Jewish literature, and therefore American literature, unique. These are twin coincidences which I believe are important to an evaluation of American literature and its development, certainly to a review of American Jewish writers and their place in American letters.

American literature is a young literature. In the measure of human history, America itself is a young country, and American literature is much younger than the country. From the beginning of the American adventure there were, of course, writers, and not a few of them are men of significant achievement: Hawthorne, for example, and Melville, Mark Twain and Whitman, Edgar Allan Poe, honored more in other countries than at home, and James, who chose to leave home for another country. The total product of American literary creativity, however, did not achieve, nor did it merit, recognition as a significant contribution to world literature. Only in the twentieth century did American literature begin to establish itself as a world literature, so much so that in a recent issue the *Times Literary Supplement* noted that if in the past the flow in the world of letters and culture was from Europe westward, today it must be admitted that the flow is from America eastward.

Now what is striking to my mind is that the emergence of the American Jewish writer coincides exactly with the coming of age, so to speak, of American letters. American literature, thus, is the only national literature in the world in which Jews were active participants during that period in which it took on its national character and developed as a major literary force in the world. There are undoubtedly many reasons which can be put forth to explain this unique happening, but what I feel is important, and the point I wish to stress, is that the Jewish writer emerged on the American scene as a creative force at a time when our country's literature itself began to develop, and, thus had the opportunity to have an impact upon, and influence, that literature in a manner which was not given to Jews in any other literature.

This is not to say that there were no Jewish writers, some quite important, in other countries and in other languages. The Jews in medieval Spain, as already mentioned, were prolific contributors to that country's letters, as were the Jews in early Renaissance Italy. Individuals, too, made significant artistic contributions, Heine in Germany is but one example, but essentially Jews were not in at the beginning of, and could not play an important role in the formative stages of, a national literature as could the American Jewish writer.

What to me seems to be equally striking, and this is the second of the two coincidences, is that the Jew begins to emerge not only as a contributor but also as a character in American fiction at the very same time. One does not enter the lists lightly against Leslie Fiedler, who has identified Jewish characters in early American works, and indeed, Jewish characters walk through American literature well before the twentieth century. But, I submit, the Jew as a major and full-bodied, often symbolic character, and Jewish life as legitimate, and indeed as indigenous, American subject matter begin to appear in the work of non-Jews as well as Jews only in the twentieth century, coinciding with the emergence of major Jewish creative talents.

It can be argued that there exists a causal relationship between the fact that American literature began to take itself, and to be taken, seriously, and the fact that Jews began to create and that Jewish figures began to appear in it at the same time. I will not pursue that argument here, but I do propose that this coincidence in American literary history does deserve consideration. To go even further, while I make no claim for causality in this historical coincidence, I am convinced that many of the special qualities which mark American literature are a direct result of the fact that Jewish writers had an opportunity to place their imprint on it at a crucial stage in its development.

Let me here interject two cautionary statements which I make even as I recognize that they may be unnecessary. It is to be understood that if in discussing a particular quality mention is made of a specific work or author, it is not to argue that that quality is central or even major in the work or to the author. The mention comes only to serve as illustration of works in which the quality can be discerned, and of authors who reflect it in their writings. Similarly, no claim of exclusivity is put forth. I do not agree that only Jewish writers exhibit a particular quality, nor do I claim that these are exclusively Jewish qualities, not to be found in the work of non-Jewish writers. The intent is simply to point to qualities found in the works of Jewish authors which spring out of and are traceable to Jewish heritage and tradition.

The Jewish tradition manifests itself in American literature, broadly speaking, in two ways, one more easily descried and noted, the second more subtle, less tangible. The first draws largely upon the Jewish experience in America, and can be said to manifest itself as substance. The second, a projection of the shaping force of tradition working within the writer, can be said to manifest itself as form. The former gives us to understand subject matter and theme in American Jewish writing, the latter helps us map the particular dimensions to which American literature has been pushed by the tradition within which the Jewish writer creates.

American Jewish literature has concentrated upon some very significant aspects of the American experience, but also significant are those chapters in American history which are not drawn upon by American Jewish writers, chapters which have shaped and determined the American psyche. The conquest of the West, for example, has generated little interest among American Jewish writers. What many regard as the most traumatic experience in American history, the Civil War, for another example, is almost nonexistent in American Jewish writing. As crucial as the Civil War may have been for America, it did not reverberate in American Jewish creativity. Chronology by itself, pointing out that massive Jewish immigration to the United States began after these events had become history, does not satisfactorily explain this fact. First, Jews did, of course, join other Americans in the move westward, and Jews did, of course, fight in the Civil War—in the Union and Confederate armies. Second, one does not need to live through a period in order to find in it raw material for the creative imagination. Faulkner and Stephen Crane, each in his own way, used the Civil War to give expression to his inner vision, as did many others who were not participants in that war. Apparently, then, in choosing materials appropriate for expressing their view of life or reaction to the world in which they live, Jewish writers did not find in these periods fitting matter.

Similarly, Jewish writers seldom set their stories in rural America. They are chroniclers of life in urban America, in the main, of life in the great metropolises of the East; rarely is the South a setting for them.

As the twentieth century began, Irving Howe notes, America began to undergo

a change of mood and consciousness that still shapes our lives. The
legacy of blood from the Civil War; the growth of ugly, soul-breaking
cities; the spread of corruption; the entry of millions of immigrants
assigned to the donkey-work of society; the recognition in short, that
this country too must bear the pains of a rampant capitalism and the
shocks of class war, all lead to a new view of things.[6]

It was at this turn in American history, when the United States
moved to confront history instead of trying "an end run past" it, that
the Jewish writer moves strongly into the mainstream of American
letters. This new mood was one which the Jew, who always lived in
history, could share and to which he could respond. Thus, the
arrival of great numbers of Jewish immigrants coincided with a new
thrust in American life to which the Jew could respond naturally. It
is to this America that Jewish writers responded, and it is in the
literature they created that we can discover the ways in which Jewish
tradition contributed to the development of American letters.

First, let us turn our attention to subject matter and theme.

We have come to characterize ourselves as a nation of immigrants.
The immigrant experience is central to American life and culture
and has had a shaping impact on it. It is acknowledged that the
immigrant experience—what it means to be an immigrant, to come
to the shores of the United States and struggle with outer reality and
inner conflict—has been most effectively summed up in the work of
Abraham Cahan in *The Rise of David Levinsky*. The immigrant
experience, for the Jew, and as depicted in Cahan's work, began in
the 1880s, with the great exodus of Jews from Eastern Europe.
There were Jews in this country from earliest colonial times. They
were among the first to settle on these shores. But Jews came in
significant numbers and began to create a Jewish culture on this
continent only with the 1880s and 1890s. This experience we find
most graphically projected in *The Rise of David Levinsky*, which traces
the growth to manhood, of a young immigrant boy thrown into a
new culture, his struggle to find meaning, and himself, through
severe inner turmoil.

The novel projects not only a Jewish experience but the
experience of any immigrant. Written by a Jew about Jews caught in

a typical Jewish trial, *The Rise of David Levinsky* captures the essentials
of the American immigrant experience: arrival and entry into a New
World; encounters, painful and rewarding, with a new way of life;
ultimate integration, with varying success, into American society.
Education is one of the magic portals through which the immigrants
can force entry (unfortunately the verb is descriptive of the nature of
the experience for many) into this new and alien culture, so protean
in its nature and so hard to define, and so unlike the European
cultures which the immigrants knew, Russian or German or French.
It is not surprising that Cahan, responding to the traditional Jewish
attitude to learning, chose the educational pull as a fitting
countervailing force in Levinsky's struggle to become an American.
Levinsky finds himself forced to choose between learning—the
traditional—and success in business—the new. Counterposing these
two value systems, Cahan succeeds in pointing to the psychological
as well as physical forces which pull at the immigrant. The struggle,
vividly portrayed, also permits Cahan to fully suggest the tragedy
inherent in the immigrant experience, for victory inevitably brings
with it the loss of great cultural treasures, and possibly of the sense of
self.

Another view of this American experience is given by Henry Roth
in his novel *Call It Sleep*, an acknowledged masterpiece periodically
revived, which has never won wide readership. A richly symbolic
work, it focuses on an immigrant youngster's encounter with the
New World and the tearing struggle he undergoes as school and
street bring him to realize that he must break away from his parents
in order to find his true self. His parents, he comes to recognize, will
never fully acclimate themselves to the new environment as he will,
but still he cannot reject them. He wants to stay with them, his
brutish father as well as his sensitive and understanding mother,
even as he moves away from them.

Cahan and Roth, like other Jewish writers, described intensely
Jewish experiences which are at the same time significantly American.
They see things through Jewish eyes, use Jewish life and customs as
their raw materials, and yet deal with an essentially American
experience. As John Higham wrote in his introduction to the Harper
Torchbook edition of *The Rise of David Levinsky*, "Cahan brought to

bear an extraordinary fusion. . . . His theme of success was distinctively American. . . . His subject matter was Jewish . . ."

The immigrant experience, and the immigrant novel, is still with us today. *Ragtime* by D. L. Doctorow, is such a retelling of the immigrant experience. It covers more, but it reaches back into history to talk about what it was like to be a Jewish immigrant, and how the Jew wove himself into the fabric of American life. Doctorow's decision not to use names for his characters, but to call the members of the American family "Mother," "Father," "Younger Brother," and members of the Jewish family by Yiddish equivalents—"Tatta," "Momma"—suggests the universality of the experiences they live through. It is in keeping with his purpose to capture the totality of the immigrant experience, which helped pattern American life and remains central to that life.

Another related theme has moved many American Jewish writers—the challenge of growing up in America. This, in a sense, is the immigrant problem moved on to the next generation. What is it like to be an American Jewish boy or girl, the child of immigrants, but not oneself an immigrant? What conflicts does one experience? How does one adjust? Growing up in Brooklyn occupies Daniel Fuchs in his trilogy composed of *Summer in Williamsburg, Homage to Blenholt*, and *Low Company*. In *The Old Bunch*, Meyer Levin writes of Jewish Chicago as James T. Farrell did for the Irish in that city in his *Lonigan Trilogy*. Attacked violently by many as a prime example of the literature of self-hate, and considered by others to be "a genuine aesthetic achievement,"[7] Michael Gold's *Jews Without Money*, one of the most effective of the proletarian novels written in America, is a searing study of a young Jewish boy growing up American on the Lower East Side of Manhattan. All of these, and many more Jewish novels, probe the ache of the children of immigrants adjusting to the American culture. They differ widely in their conclusions on how to ease the ache and respond to the inner needs. Some, like Roth, suggest that one can find one's way within the Jewish tradition, and others, like Michael Gold, insist that ease can be found only by throwing away Jewish tradition, but all focus on the same matter and share a common theme.

These works deal with Jews and Jewish life, and clearly spring out of the Jewishness of the writers, but they touch central experiences in American life, experiences which test the foundations upon which America rests. They attempt to capture and translate into human terms the pressures which shape non-Jewish as well as Jewish life in the American crucible. America is, in good part, an outgrowth of those tensions within our society which beset Jews in this country, and Jewish writers were drawn to explore and probe their significance and the forces and tensions they released. Why were these matters so important to the Jews, perhaps more important than to others? Is there something in the Jewish tradition which made this so? To these questions I will return a little later.

There is another dimension to the Jewish contribution to American letters that strikes us and which is projected in these works—they are all urban novels. The Jewish voice in American literature is very largely, if not exclusively, the voice of the city. We do not find Jewish writers dealing with rural America, with country, farming, mining areas. Here there is a novel of the South, there a work set in New England, and elsewhere one set in a small plains town, or an academic village in the West, but almost exclusively the Jewish writer's milieu is the city. The Jewish suburban novel, which has begun to appear with frequency, is, of course, literally an extension of urban life.

The face of America upon which the Jewish writer concentrates is the metropolitan face. It is true that for some, American history is seen as movement off the land into the cities, and all aspects of American life are explained in terms of the growth of the cities and the impact of that movement on the quality of life, temper of thought, and growth of the spirit. Steven Marcus recently pointed out that there is a particular subculture in which the American Jew seems to be totally engulfed.[8] He calls it the subculture of city life, particularly New York City life. It is not only the general urban experience but a particular city, New York City, that in his view serves as the center of American Jewish creativity. Civic loyalty may lead to argument—Chicago, for example, may feel entitled to recognition not much less than that which Marcus assigns to New York—but what remains is the centrality of the urban experience in American Jewish letters. Again we have to ask: Is this an outgrowth of the Jewish tradition? Is there something within this experience that speaks particularly to Jews? Whatever the answer may be, and I will try to explore this soon, here, too, American Jewish writers touch upon a very significant aspect of American life.

A third area draws attention. American Jewish writers deal with what I would call the "American conflict." Life in the United States seems to force confrontations. This has been noted by many observers of American life, and led to serious comment by Tocqueville, among others. This "American conflict" expresses itself in many ways, but essentially it can be said to be the conflict between the ideal and the real.

America grew out of a great ideal, a great dream, but in life the ideal continually bruises itself against the hard realities. This constant clash is the inevitable struggle that rises out of the tension between tradition and progress, the conflict between the old and the new. The nation was built by immigrants who brought with them old traditions even as they chose a new place to live. They felt the exhilaration that comes from leaving the old and creating everything anew, and yet, one cannot easily unload the baggage of the ages. For them the age-old conundrum of how to reconcile the old with the new became a question of life. Can one transplant anything from the Old World in this new Golden Land?

This vexing question manifests itself in many ways: in the conflict between culture and business, humanitarian concerns and industrial needs, worker and machine, and in personal terms for writers, this is the conflict between the artist and society. The artist in his mind always stands for the ideal—for culture, for art, for the questing creative urge—as opposed to the real—business, industry, the conservative drag which seeks to restrain imaginative flight. This conflict is central in the work of American Jewish writers. Thematically it is often projected as the war between generations, fathers against sons, and sons against fathers; the young trying to break away from the old, the new striving to break beyond the bonds set by tradition. In some ways this is a repetition of the plight of the second generation of immigrants, but in its later development it revolves less around the question of practices and more around the question of values, rejection by the young of the traditional values and philosophies of their parents in favor of new attitudes and visions. This theme runs through the writings of author after author, Isaac Rosenfeld, Norman Mailer, Philip Roth, and J. D. Salinger, to name just a few. In nearly all cases these authors project the conflict in Jewish terms, but they touch on a central concern in American life.

This conflict grew more intense, and at mid-century the shadow of alienation moved darkly across America. The tensions and stresses which flowed from it seemed in some ways to be merely a recasting of earlier agonies. The war between the fathers and the sons was now seen as a generation gap; the rejection of accepted beliefs and values was shouted forth in slogans for peace now and an end to pollution; wrenching free from established familial and societal structures was demonstrated by dropping-out and freaking-out. The conflict, however, cut more deeply, as evidenced by the violence, physical and emotional, which flared up. Edward Wallant, Allen Ginsberg, and Bernard Malamud are representative of the many Jewish writers whose voices cried out bitterly at the destruction of human relationships and the erosion of feeling which led to loneliness, frustration, and alienation.

It has been pointed out that alienation came to the United States with its earliest settlers. The Pilgrims came to these shores as to a Promised Land, but they were faced by a hostile and forbidding wilderness which heightened their sense of exile, aliens in a strange and unwelcoming environment. But the contemporary sense of alienation is not the same as that felt by earlier generations, even if the two share elements in common, and the cry it has wrung from twentieth-century writers is a bitter and angry one. For those seeking symbols to convey the rage and fear of the alienated, the Jew—the prototypical figure of exile, the outsider even in societies in which he was a long-time sojourner, the figure who stood not only outside but against the society in which he lived—was a natural, almost inevitable choice. For the Jew himself, especially the American Jew, who had permitted himself the hope that at last here he would become a native son, to be riven again by a sense of alienation was a double anguish, and Jewish American writers have uttered some of the most piercing and angry denunciations against the conditions that drive the sensitive and the young and the creative out of the mainstream, or off the main streets, of life. They, after all, as Isaac Rosenfeld poignantly noted in *An Age of Enormity*, are "specialists in alienation."

Among the most effective portrayers of modern alienated man is J. D. Salinger. *Catcher in the Rye* was recognized as their *cri de coeur* by the old as well as the young. Holden's breakdown is moving and tearing beyond the fact that it details the wounding of a young soul. It reaches us because it describes the dissolution of the bonds which tie the human soul to its fellow-soul, man to his fellow-man. It decries not alone the widening gap between children and parents, youth and adults, but the loss by man of his ability to relate to other human beings and to the world he inhabits.

The response to alienation given by writers such as Salinger and Mailer and Rosenfeld and Ginsberg is active rejection of the established ways. For some, the more violent and destructive the rejection, the more positive the response. There are, however, others who see a different way, and that way is return to the true core of tradition. They, too, sense the alienation and want to reestablish the vital human contacts, but rejection and violence, to them, only deepen alienation. The way out of the loneliness and frustration is to turn back to the tradition, find the truth which is there embedded, and, strengthened by exposure to it, bring vitality to human relations. Cynthia Ozick and Hugh Nissenson are examples of these reaffirmers of the need to allow the tradition to work its good in the world instead of trying to destroy it. Other examples of this response are represented by Charles Angoff, in his multi-volumed saga of the Polansky family, and by Chaim Potok, who returns to the same story; both depict the struggle of the traditionally committed to fight through alienation, find revival in the waters of their heritage, and live with the tension created by the contemporary world and the ancient tradition. This response reflects not only Jewish belief or loyalty, but also an American attitude which calls for a reaffirmation of the ideals upon which America was built as the answer to the challenges modern society, built on those ideals, has to face.

An insight into the Jewishness of these writers, even when they most strongly demand to be seen not as Jews but as Americans, is granted us by Philip Roth. Roth has steadily and vociferously declared that he does not speak as a Jew, that he does not see himself as a Jew, and doesn't want to be seen as a Jew. Recently he reported on a visit to Europe. He decided to visit the haunts of Kafka, whom he greatly admired. He walked the streets of Prague, he tells, and suddenly,

> I understood that a connection of sorts existed between myself and this place; here was one of those dense corners of Jewish Europe which Hitler had emptied of Jews, a place which in earlier days must have been not too unlike those neighborhoods of Austro-Hungarian Hamburg and Czarist Kiev, where the two branches of my own family had lived before their emigration to America at the beginning of the century. Looking for Kafka's landmarks I had, to my surprise, come upon some landmarks that felt to me like my own.[9]

The sudden realization by Roth that he, despite his disclaimers, is not entirely free of the history of his people, the traditions of his past, is an announcement on his part that history and tradition have always shaped his creative achievements. Without enlarging too much on this point, I would suggest that Roth's discovery of the roots of his being is part of the heightened awareness of their Jewishness which has manifested itself among Jewish writers. Some attribute this to the establishment of a Jewish state in Israel. I, on the other hand, feel that Israel has played a small part in this identification of themselves as Jews by Jewish writers. It is the Holocaust and its impact on modern man, I suggest, that has reached into their consciousness and brought them to realize that it was their Jewish tradition that was expressing itself in their writings even as they declared themselves independent of it.

The self-expression of gifted sensitive people does not spring full-grown from under the creative pen, independent of its creator's roots. It springs out of beginnings, and these are intangibles. Not so easily pinned down or pointed to, they are as much a part of the artist as his immediate sensory experiences. The writer creates not only with his artistic gifts but also out of his heritage. American Jewish writers spin their work out of their American experiences, but it is shaped and flavored by their Jewish roots. The immigrant experience, urban life, certainly the Holocaust, are significantly Jewish experiences, and they are also American, indeed universal, experiences. The Jewish writer who treats these matters may approach them in their universal aspects, but in the last analysis, how he treats them is determined by the traditions which exist and have existed within the Jewish culture upon which he was nurtured. This is the more subtle manner, to which I referred above, in which Jewish tradition expresses itself in American Jewish letters.

Let us take, for an example, the matter of style. One of the most significant impacts Jewish writers have had on American literature, I suggest, is in the development of style. There has been developed and preserved among Jews, transmitted from generation to generation, a deeply rooted reverence for the word. The word as an act of creation is central in the Jewish tradition, and thus a sacredness attaches to the word. The Jew regards the word written, certainly, and even the word spoken, with a particular reverence. This sense, transmitted as part of his cultural heritage to the Jewish writer, has had a recognizable effect on American writing. Let me illustrate.

In the period between World War I and World War II the pervasive force in American literature was Ernest Hemingway. Hemingway was a towering figure in American literature in many ways, and clearly the Hemingway style was the style that held American literature entrammeled. Generations of students were sent to the Hemingway well to imbibe the principles of effective writing. Professors of freshman composition used up their red pencils to teach those on the threshold of their cultural majority the Hemingway lesson: write taut, muscular prose; cut out adjectives; reduce the total number of words, and you heighten the impact, the force, of your writing. This influence cut deeply and held fast. Few dared to stand against it, and only men of great original creativity escaped it.

The one who succeeded in breaking Hemingway's hold on American style was Saul Bellow. Saul Bellow reestablished the respectability of rhetoric in American letters with the appearance of *The Adventures of Augie March*, a picaresque novel in which he celebrates language. Matching Augie's exuberance of spirit and joy of life is a soaring, tumbling, joyous river of language. Language is not pared and controlled, it is let loose to run free in the world to create.

The influence of Jewish writers on style is not limited to Bellow's work. Joseph Heller broke new ground with *Catch 22*, and Alter finds that out of his early milieu Malamud created not only a new style, but a new technique. Nor is it all in the past. E. L. Doctorow's new novel *Ragtime* has been accorded extravagant praise. What its ultimate place in American letters will be, time will determine, but it has been hailed initially for its attempt at a stylistic breakthrough. It strives for a particularly and peculiarly American style, attempting to translate what is perhaps the only indigenous American cultural development, jazz, into language, translating from music into literature. Doctorow's aim is to create a new prose—ragtime prose. Interestingly, and perhaps not purely as a coincidence, *Ragtime*, written in this new special rhythmic pattern, is, as already mentioned, an immigrant novel. Joining form to substance we must conclude that Doctorow is suggesting, with his intermeshing of subject matter and style, that the immigrant experience—a Jewish experience, the "greener" agonizing his way into American life—is the essential American experience, as American as ragtime, as American as jazz.

This leads to another manifestation of the Jewish tradition in American literature. Following on the consideration of style and a predilection for rich, flowing, evocative language, it might seem to be paradoxical, except for the fact that in the tradition from which it springs, it stands together with the word.

Bellow and other Jewish writers became spokesmen for rational man, advocates of reason, returning intelligence and cerebration to American literature. In this, too, they stand against Hemingway, but not only Hemingway. Fitzgerald, for example, and Thomas Wolfe distrusted reason, and Faulkner's people are moved by dark, inexpressible emotions rather than intellect. Their disciples were anti-intellectuals who gave the term "egghead" its derisive and opprobious connotations and preached a distrust of human reason. Through his characters Hemingway argues that one should rely on, and react in accordance with, one's gut feelings, with the impulses which rise out of one's innards, in coping with the world. Human reason is inadequate, in his doctrine, and can only lead us into unnaturalness. It is not surprising that opposed to Jake Barnes, a model Hemingway hero, stands Robert Cohn. The reaction against this attitude in literature, and the return to reason in literature, was led by Bellow and people like him.

These two central and basic concepts, a sense of the independent life, if not sacredness, of the word, and commitment to the primacy of reason in determining human action, a sense that reason is the glory of the man, and that that glory finds its richest fulfilment in the word, came to the Jewish writer as naturally as his mother's milk. They are part of the tradition which has inspired Jewish life over the centuries and which begins to be transmitted to the Jewish child with the cradle songs from which he learns to speak his first words. Indeed, in developing a scale of the living universe, the talmudic sages called the lowest, the mineral stage, *domem*—non-speaking— and man, the highest stage of all, *medaber*—a maker of words.

These two basic concepts are interrelated in the Jewish tradition, for they spring from an even more fundamental and embracing belief, which in the eyes of some is the cornerstone on which the entire Jewish tradition rests. This is the basic principle of the sacredness of the human spirit.[10] Every human carries within him a spark that is not man, but is, rather, a particle of the divine within man. By carrying himself in awareness that he is a vessel containing this spark of divinity, man becomes a partner with the Almighty in creation, a fulfiller of the divine function on earth. This view of man lies beneath and indeed animates the artistic creations of many American Jewish writers; of Bellow, certainly of Bernard Malamud, and of younger writers such as Cynthia Ozick and Hugh Nissenson, young writers who boldly confront themselves and the American society in which they live, and ask; What is it that makes life worth living? What is it that makes man, man; and me, me? What is it that can give meaning to the American experience? The answer which their work suggests they give to these questions is a return to this concept of the sacredness of human life.

This is not to suggest that these writers are necessarily observant or even professing Jews, nor does it mean that they expressly have accepted this concept. Fiedler has already noted that much of

American Jewish literature springs out of a religious impulse, even when it is "a frantic religiosity without God."[11] Similarly, Irving Mallin has suggested that all Jewish writers write out of a strictly religious impulse, that fundamentally American Jewish creativity is theological, is really an expression of the Jewish religion. Even those who strike out against the Jewish religion, who throw over the traditions of their fathers and reject Judaism, he argues, do so out of a religious impulse. Theirs is not the secular radicalism which has driven others, but rather a religious radicalism which has driven them out of Judaism because it does not slake their religious thirst. Through all their writing, he concludes, they seek a religious fulfillment, which is an outgrowth of the Jewish heritage. Perhaps Mallin goes far, but only a little. Examine *Catch 22*. This novel, one of the most significant to come out of World War II, is in essence a celebration of the sacredness of human life. Heller's verbal pyrotechnics as well as his wild humor spring out of an essentially religious vision, and are a reaction against the dehumanization of man and the denial of the sacredness of human life and of the human spirit. Note again, parenthetically, that Heller developed a rich, rolling style which glorifies, and glories in, words, something that manifests itself again in his latest novel, *Something Happened*.

The inner, traditionally Jewish view of man, which moves within Heller, also moves so many American Jewish writers, and informs so many of their works. The American Jewish writer is driven by a moral imperative, and his work is an attempt to project the moral questions posed by modern life, as Josephine Knapp, basing herself largely on Landis's "code of *mentshlekhkayt*," has argued expansively. This, of course, is not true only of Jewish writers, but it seems to be the predominant theme in their writings, and the questions that concern them seem to have a particularly Jewish resonance. This is the red thread that runs through all the works mentioned, beginning with *The Rise of David Levinsky*.

The irony contained in the very title, *The Rise of David Levinsky*, underscores the major moral dilemma Cahan sees emerging from the move of European Jewry to America. The rise of David Levinsky, Cahan declares, is the destruction of David Levinsky. His rise culminates in his becoming a millionaire, but the cost is the destruction of his soul. Levinsky left his *shtetel* a *yeshiva bochur*, filled with a respect and a love for learning and the knowledge that in devoting himself to Torah he would fulfill himself as well as the Jewish ideal. Arrived in America, he finds himself torn between his traditional ideal and the lure of the new American dream. This confrontation is projected through the decision Levinsky must make: Shall he continue the Jewish ideal of learning (recast into its new form of a tuition-free college education, and the prospect of attaining to the post of a lowly college instructor, the American equivalent of the Yiddish *batlan*), or shall he become a successful businessman? He chooses to become a businessman, succeeds to the nth degree, and this is his rise; but this rise is, in truth, his fall. Throughout his life, even as financial conquests increase, he is haunted by the realization that he was false to the trust placed in him by his mother. It was she who carried and cared for him, and finally gave up her life to save his, for her dream was that he would grow up to be a man of the mind, a man of the spirit. For this ideal his mother was prepared to sacrifice herself, rushing forward to be destroyed. Levinsky's rise—the great American success symbol, becoming a millionaire—was a betrayal of his mother's life's dream, and his life, literally and metaphysically, is thereby rendered sterile. With him his line comes to an end.

This theme, in varying forms, runs throughout American Jewish writing. Constantly posed is the heart-riving question: Why is it necessary to sell one's soul in this American environment? That the soul must be sold is foregone, in the view of Jewish writers, and their writings, regardless of the individual responses they give, underscore this view of the American Jewish experience. For whatever reason, they find that the Jewish tradition out of which they come, and the culture and values of the New World, are inimical, and for most of them, in this inevitable clash, the old tradition gives way; it cannot withstand the onslaught of American life. Paradoxically, this is viewed not as a victory for American life, but as a defeat, for though it has the power to destroy the old, America cannot replace it with something of equal value, of equal spiritual value, to keep life meaningful and worthwhile.

A despairing cry wrung from the Jewish American writer over this result of Americanization is one of the chief characteristics of

American Jewish fiction. It is powerful and poignant because it issues ultimately not as a denial of life, not in a negative form, but in a positive form, as a reaffirmation of faith in life and its promise. American Jewish writers, when all is said and done, are almost always yea-sayers, bruised and bloodied perhaps, but still optimistic, and what they reaffirm is the acceptance of the essence of the ancient tradition from which they have emerged. Even those who are moved to attack the tradition most fiercely, attack it because they feel that it has fallen into rigidified conventions which obscure its shining essence, and distance from it its feeling and sensitive young.

Mr. Sammler, in Bellow's novel, sums up his understanding of his, and every man's, true situation on this planet, and I am sure that Bellow heard clearly the talmudic echoes in the statement as he put it down. Mr. Sammler debates man and life with Dr. V. Govinda Lal, the Hindu professor of physics who proposes colonizing the moon, and "who must have been sick of earth to begin with . . . and partly he was right" (p. 177). True, ṣays Mr. Sammler, "When you know what pain is, you agree that not to have been born is better. But being born one respects the powers of creation, one obeys the will of God—with whatever inner reservations truth imposes."[12] This is almost word for word a dispute recorded in the Talmud. The Academy of Hillel and the Academy of Shamai for two and a half years debated the question of whether it would have been better for man not to have been created at all, and came to the conclusion that though it would have been better for man not to have been created, now that he has been created let him pay attention to his deeds.[13]

In this connection we can recall that when *Herzog* first appeared, critics were divided over the question of whether the novel ends with a yea or with a nay, does it offer a positive or negative conclusion concerning man and life? Many concluded that *Herzog* was a pessimistic book and ended with a bleak view of man. Over the years the view has changed, and it is now acknowledged that when Moses Herzog finally lies down on his Recamier couch, he is not retreating from the world but preparing to embrace it. Here, too, Bellow is saying that life may be frightening, its realities may be terrifying, but the human spirit can rise above the fright and the terror and make the world, and life, beautiful and good.

The clash between the Jewish psyche and the American reality, this ever-recurring theme in American Jewish literature, is strikingly developed in Saul Mallof's novel, *Heartland*. A Jewish writer is invited to join in an annual artistic festival at a women's college in the Rocky Mountains. How he fares, and what happens to him on this campus, is not only Mallof's story, but his symbolically evoked vision of the Jew in America. *Heartland* is at once the American heartland, the land of the poet's heart, and the arena where the fateful battle for the soul of America is joined.

Under its cultural and enlightened surface—a festival of the arts sponsored by a liberal arts college for women in America's most awesome mountain fastness—says Mallof, America at heart is still given over to darkness and violence, to a paganism which is the denial of the truly good and bright in life. Brought into this environment, the burnt-out writer from the canyons of Manhattan—the prototypical Jewish *schlemiel*—reasserts himself amid the alien forbidding peaks of the land and the dark irrational recesses of the heart, to reaffirm the beauty of life and the need for every human being to struggle through a harsh and difficult world to find and bestow goodness. The primitive mountain spirit seems to oppose the communal and social moral responsibility which his Jewish soul requires, and he returns to the East, where life may be hard but is not pagan. This, in its American form, is for the Jewish writer a reenactment of Jacob's night-long wrestling with the dark enemy. It is a distinctly Jewish encounter, but it mirrors with frightening accuracy an essential American struggle.

The works mentioned grapple with serious matters; it is therefore all the more striking that almost without exception they are cast in the comic mold. Many have celebrated Jewish humor, which is explained as a strategy for survival. Faced with hatred, harshness, physical annihilation—which has been his experience in the world—the Jew has developed a humor which combines wit, irony, and self-deprecation, and serves at once as a shield against, and a response to, the despair and bitterness which fear and persecution bring. If the humor of the Jew is his response to the discrepancy between his inner world and outer reality—the source of humor—then not unnaturally, his humor becomes more intense and extreme as that discrepancy grows. "Black humor" has certainly become one of the major modes of American literary expression, and some of the blackest and most comic of the black humorists have been Jews. The humorous mode has become part of the Jewish tradition, particularly through the folk reactions of East European Jews and the works of Yiddish humorists, and this, too, has been transplanted to American soil. The Jew, says Professor Gillman, has brought to American literature "a furious wit."[14] Joseph Heller, Stanley Elkin, Bruce Jay Friedman, Wallace Markfield are representative of the school, but its strains run through Bellow and Malamud and Roth, and hark back to the grotesques found in Nathaniel West and Daniel Fuchs.

Let me close with one more observation, to my mind a striking one, which emerges from a study of American Jewish writing. The Jewish writer is most likely to succeed creatively, artistically, when he most directly faces up to himself and his situation as an American—read man—with roots within an ancient tradition—read Jew; he is most likely to fail when he tries to avoid or deny his background and his tradition. There are exceptions, of course. Bernard Malamud, for example, has written what may very well be the best American baseball novel, a work that makes use of the national pastime as a metaphor of the American spirit, and the novel, his first, titled *The Natural*, draws not at all on Jewish materials or subject matter. Others can be pointed out as having produced significant works without drawing upon their Jewish tradition for subject matter or theme. In the main, however, Jewish writers have written best when they have written out of their Jewishness, and have done their poorest work when they have tried to escape it. "When Jews are *directly* concerned with their Jewishness," asserts Irving Mallin, "they produce powerful, sincere art; when they are not, they offer less intense, phony, or imperfect work." A classic example is Philip Roth.

Philip Roth is a major talent who has not achieved the level to which that talent should have brought him. There seems to be a direct relationship between his successful work and his acceptance of his Jewishness. I speak, of course, not about his convictions or practices, but about his point of view, his attitude, and I speak about him as a writer. Those works he has turned out which have merit are works in which he was prepared to confront himself head-on as a Jew. *Portnoy's Complaint*, which made many Jews unhappy, his overly long novel, *Letting Go*, the collection of stories which brought him his first and greatest acclaim, *Goodbye Columbus*, were flawed to a greater or lesser degree, but they represent his best work. In all of them he confronts himself as a Jew. He draws his material from his Jewish background and deals with problems and situations which confront Jews, and he deals with them from the point of view of their Jewish protagonists. His other works, which he has tried to keep free of Jewish matter or overtones, are at a much lower level.

I believe I understand what Roth is trying to say when he demands that he be viewed not as a Jewish writer but as an American writer. His error is his failure to recognize that by denying that which is natural within him he does not make himself more American. To the contrary; by trying to suppress his Jewishness he turns away from that which will permit him to best express himself artistically and is best calculated to permit his native talent to create well. Willy-nilly he must write about his experiences as he responds to them, which is to say as a Jew, and he can give himself the strongest artistic base by accepting his Jewishness and working out of it. When he has refused to confront himself as a Jew, he has failed as an American, not only as a Jewish, artist. Perhaps this is what he came to recognize when he walked through the streets of Prague in the footsteps of Kafka.

Similarly, Leslie Fiedler suggests that Lionel Trilling, a major figure, failed artistically in his novel *The Middle of the Journey* because he chose not to make his protagonist a Jew. And is it only coincidental that *Henderson the Rain King* is Bellow's weakest book?

Jewishness has a strange and obstinate way of asserting itself, even when it is not openly acknowledged. Readers of *Catcher in the Rye* sense that Holden Caulfield is a West Side Jewish adolescent, despite the fact that Salinger clearly identifies him otherwise. Many literary critics, on studying Arthur Miller's *Death of a Salesman*, concluded that the play seemed to be a Jewish work, though nowhere is Loman identified as a Jew. Recently Miller admitted that he modeled the character on his uncle, whom he saw as the prototype of the salesman, and that he was talking about Jewish life and Jewish values in this classic American play.[15]

Tradition does not easily die, it fights to extrude itself in the work of the Jewish writer. In two or three succeeding generations it may disappear, but to date it is alive and vital, leaving its imprint directly and indirectly on the sons and daughters of that tradition who take up the pen. The impact these writers have had on American literature has been significant and powerful, thematically, structurally, stylistically. This is so, I submit, because the Jewish writer was able to enter into that literature early, and because he felt free to talk about himself as a Jew, less self-consciousnessly and with greater naturalness than was possible for him in the literature of any other country. He felt no inhibition in confronting general problems through his Jewish tradition, and this in turn has enabled him to greatly enrich American literature, particularly the novel and the drama, and help it reach the eminence it occupies today.

NOTES

1. Emphasis in the original.
2. *Medium*, no. 10 (December 1975–January 1976): 1–2.
3. Robert Alter, *After the Tradition*, p. 18.
4. Alvin H. Rosenfeld, "The Progress of the American Jewish Novel," *Response* no. 1 (Spring 1973): 115.
5. Leslie Fiedler, *The Collected Essays of Leslie Fiedler*, vol. 2 (New York: Stein & Day, 1971), p. 98.
6. Irving Howe, "The American Voice—It Begins on a Note of Wonder," *New York Times Book Review*, July 4, 1976, p. 2.
7. See Michael Harrington's "Afterword" to the Avon Library edition, 1965.
8. *New York Times Book Review*, February 8, 1976, p. 2.
9. *New York Times Book Review*, February 15, 1976, p. 6.
10. A full exposition of this concept in Judaism, and how it permeates every aspect of Jewish law and tradition, is given by Samuel Belkin, *In His Image* (New York: Abelard-Schuman, 1960).
11. Fiedler, op. cit., p. 90.
12. Saul Bellow, *Mr. Sammler's Planet* (New York: Viking Press, 1970), p. 223.
13. Babylonian Talmud, *Erubin* 136b.
14. Richard Gillman, in *New York Times*, July 17, 1975.
15. Cf. Sig Altman, *The Comic Image of the Jew* (Rutherford, N. J.: Fairleigh Dickinson University Press, 1971), p. 52.

SELECTED BIBLIOGRAPHY

Allen, Walter. *The Modern Novel in Britain and the United States*. New York: E.P. Dutton, 1964.
Alter, Robert. *After the Tradition: Essays on Modern Jewish Writing*. New York: E. P. Dutton, 1971.
Altman, Sig. *The Comic Image of the Jew*. Rutherford, N. J.; Fairleigh Dickinson University Press, 1971.
Fiedler, Leslie. *The Collected Essays of Leslie Fiedler*. New York: Stein & Day, 1971.
Fisch, Harold. *The Dual Image*. New York: Ktav Publishing House, 1971.
Guttman, Allen. *The Jewish Writer in America: Assimilation and the Crisis of Identity*. New York: Oxford University Press, 1971.
Howe, Irving. *World of Our Fathers*. New York: Harcourt Brace Jovanovich, 1976.
Kazin, Alfred. *Contemporaries*. Boston: Little, Brown, 1962.
Knapp, Josephine Zadovsky. *The Trial of Judaism in Contemporary Jewish Writing*. Urbana: University of Illinois Press, 1975.
Liptzin, Solomon. *The Jew in American Literature*. New York: Bloch, 1966.
Mallin, Irving. *Jews and Americans*. Carbondale: Southern Illinois University Press, 1965.
———, ed. *Contemporary American Jewish Literature*. Bloomington: Indiana University Press, 1973.
———, and Stark, Irwin, eds. *Breakthrough: A Treasury of Contemporary American Jewish Literature*. New York: McGraw-Hill, 1964.

Mersand, Joseph. *Traditions in American Literature: A Study of Jewish Character and Authors*. Port Washington, N. Y.: Kennikat Press, 1968.

Pinsker, Sanford. *The Schlemiel as Metaphor: Studies in the Yiddish and American Novel*. Carbondale: Southern Illinois University Press, 1971.

Roth, Philip. *Reading Myself and Others*. New York: Farrar, Straus & Giroux, 1975.

Schulz, Max F. *Radical Sophistication: Studies in Contemporary Jewish-American Novelists*. Athens, Ohio: Ohio University Press, 1969.

Sherman, Bernard. *The Invention of the Jew: Jewish-American Education Novels*. New York: Thomas Yoseloff, 1969.

The Political Tradition of the American Jew

DANIEL J. ELAZAR

AT NO TIME IN American Jewish history have American Jews been more visible in the American political process than they are today, or more integrated into the American body politic. Yet at no time in American Jewish history have American Jews been more conscious of their common political interests as Jews and even—it may be said—of the political character of Jewish peoplehood. This seeming paradox lies at the heart of the political tradition of the American Jew.

The contemporary political situation of American Jews rests upon two struggles. One is the Jews' position as equal citizens in the world's greatest democratic republic, which, because it is a new society founded on modern principles, always has been open in principle to the civic and political participation of every citizen. The only struggle which Jews had in the United States was one of affirming their status as citizens. While that struggle had its moments, duly recorded in the annals of American Jewish history, by world standards it was hardly a struggle at all, over almost before it began at the time of the American Revolution.

The other foundation is the fact of the Jewish political renaissance in the twentieth century, which has led to a rediscovery of the political dimension of Jewish life. Beginning with Zionism and the effort to restore the Jewish national home, this rebirth has led an increasing number of American Jews to rediscover that being Jewish involves political interests and concerns, not to speak of the central commitment of Judaism, which is to build the holy commonwealth.

In this essay, I propose to look at one aspect of the political tradition of the American Jew, namely, the relationship between

American and Jewish political ideas, and then examine some ways in which that relationship has shaped Jewish behavior in the United States. For example, the Jew as reformer in American society—a most common role—is reflecting a secularized version of the ancient Jewish pursuit of the holy commonwealth transposed onto the American scene, and in many cases is also working to protest the liberal society which has enabled individual Jews to become full and good citizens. The two dimensions of these efforts are so intermingled that they cannot be separated accurately.

Though classical American political thought owes much to classical Jewish political ideas, the most that can be said of the great majority of the Jewish immigrants to America (who came here with little political knowledge or concern) is that their Jewish heritage predisposed them to be perhaps tangentially receptive to the fundamental American political ideas.[1] Moreover, those politically conscious Jews who came with formed political ideas espoused notions substantially different from those either of the United States or of classical Judaism, based as they were on continental notions of statist democracy and socialism. Finally, such political ideas as were brought from Europe by Jews of all persuasions and levels of political interest had been developed in response to the political experiences of Europe in the eighteenth and nineteenth centuries, particularly those produced by the French Revolution; experiences which ran in paths quite different from those of America. Consequently, the immigrant Jews and their descendants have had to adapt themselves to American political ideas, either as a matter of desire or simply out of necessity. That process of adaptation is now coming to an end. Its successful completion may have the paradoxical effect of bringing American Jews closer to classical Jewish political ideas (albeit unknowingly) than at any time in the past seventeen centuries.

Classical American political ideas are derived in part from the liberal "natural right" tradition, which developed as part of the scientific revolution that ushered in the modern age in the seventeenth century and the enlightenment that gave the modern age its intellectual tone in the eighteenth.[2] They are derived to an equal or greater extent from the English and American interpretations of biblical (or, in their terms, Old Testament) political ideas, particularly those of the Torah and the Former Prophets, in the same centuries.[3] Both streams came together in the formation of the United States. The former was dominant among the new nation's intellectuals of the squirearchy and the liberal professions, particularly in the Middle States and the South, and the latter was dominant among the nation's intellectuals of the church and the academy, particularly in New England and the West; but both were shared to some degree by all elements involved in the development of America from the revolutionary era until the Civil War.

For our purposes, we may identify four key idea complexes that have shaped American politics.

1. *Tradition* (as opposed to Ideology). This is the sense that there exists an American political tradition, supported by a general consensus of all Americans, within which American politics is conducted. It is to this tradition, rather than to any ideology (or ideologies), that Americans turn to justify current political interests or notions, even though crypto-ideologies may exist on the American scene from time to time. In practical terms, this reliance on tradition allows Americans to be pragmatic in their approach to specific political problems, at least up to the boundaries of the tradition itself. It also discourages the advance formulation of grand programs.[4]

2. *Agrarianism* (as opposed to Urbanity). American political values, in their original form, look to the vision of a commonwealth that supports and encourages the agrarian virtues of individual self-reliance and family solidarity within the framework of a cooperative community, and the agrarian ideals of classlessness (or minimal class distinctions), religiosity, and ownership of private property by those somehow involved in its use. Qualities of urbanity, sophistication, and cosmopolitanism (despite their undeniable attractiveness) have been rendered secondary to the agrarian virtues when the American public has consciously faced crucial choices over the years. In practical political terms, this has meant that Americans in any given age have preferred to keep the role of government as limited as possible, but as active as necessary, to maximize the possibilities of individual freedom, opportunity, and choice, and to help maintain life-styles that reflect agrarian values.[5]

3. *Federalism* (as opposed to Centralism). Federalism is the fundamental principle governing the structure and process of government in the United States. The federal idea of individuals and communities linked by a constitution or covenant, under the rule of law, in such a way that each member of the covenanting community retains his (or its) ultimate integrity and a measure of power under the covenant law, with its consequent political implications of power dispersed among many centers rather than concentrated (even theoretically) in one, is a principle which has been maintained in the face of many pressures over the years. In practical applications of this principle, Americans have sought to maximize local control where government has had to act, within the framework of national consensus, and to maintain a division of powers between the federal government, the states, and the local governments, even as all these separate centers of power are expected to cooperate with one another in partnership.[6]

4. *Messianism* (as opposed to Fatalism). American politics is animated by a messianic vision of the meaning of America and of the role the United States is destined to play in the improvement of humanity. This messianism is based on the notion that Americans have their own covenant with the Almighty to do good works, that they are, at the very least, what Abraham Lincoln termed an "almost chosen people." It stresses the unique character of America and its institutions, but it also encourages Americans to take an optimistic attitude regarding the possibilities for significant improvement in mankind as a whole. Thus it is politically incumbent upon Americans to use politics for such improvements at home and abroad as appear to be possible at any given time.[7]

These four elements have their roots, wholly or in part, in the political ideas of the Bible. The ancient Israelite tribal confederacy was bound together by the unique tradition of Sinai and the covenant, which demanded that the Jews maintain a polity based on agrarian virtues in order to serve as witnesses to the ultimate achievement of a messianic order of worldwide scope.[8] Most of the Jews who came to the United States were not only unacquainted with the nonbiblical sources of the American political tradition, but, despite the infusion into their lives of biblically rooted values, were further removed from a political understanding of the Bible than their non-Jewish hosts, whose school civics texts until recently cited biblical sources to justify fundamental American political ideas.[9]

Because of the circumstances of Jewish life in Europe, the overwhelming majority of the Jews arriving in America came from highly apolitical backgrounds; and nowhere were they more apolitical than in Eastern Europe, from whence the overwhelming majority of Jews came to the United States. At the time of the American Revolution, in no country in Europe had the Jews had a share in the government, either because they were excluded as Jews or simply because they came from countries where only the inner circle of the aristocracy participated in politics. However, most of the Jewish immigrants from Western and Central Europe came after their countries of origin had felt something of the impact of modern republicanism. Eastern European Jews did not have even that experience. While their communities had a substantial measure of internal autonomy, by the nineteenth century Jewish self-government had degenerated into a form of oligarchic rule in which the rabbis and the rich shared such power as the increasingly reluctant non-Jewish authorities allowed them.[10]

In the wake of the European revolutionary eruptions of the eighteenth and nineteenth centuries, some Jews had managed to acquire a limited political education—limited in the sense that it was primarily revolutionary, concerned with tearing down old regimes, but extraordinarily naive about the problems of erecting new ones or maintaining a post-revolutionary, political order. Most of their brethren, however, had to acquire political knowledge along with political experience after arriving in the United States.

Since the French Revolution (and its subsequent "heirs") gave most Jews their first opportunity to participate in politics after some seventeen centuries of exile from the political realm, the Jews became and remained partisans of that revolution, persisting in their partisanship to our own day.[11] When the Jews began their great migration to the United States at the end of the nineteenth century, they brought modifications of European revolutionary ideas with them in various guises (ranging from Jacobin liberalism to Marxism). While the American experience softened most of the more radical expressions of those ideas, they remained a strong influence even among many of the more assimilated and prosperous Jews.[12]

Comparing the political notions of the Jewish immigrants with their American counterparts, one might find that, among the politically conscious, tradition had been abandoned as a source of political ideas and replaced by ideology, particularly the ideologies of the left. The agrarian virtues and ideas had been replaced by a kind of urban liberalism based, on the one hand, on a dissatisfaction with the great socioeconomic differences between groups, and, on the other, on a desire to eliminate political distinctions between individuals. In place of federal notions, expecting the diffusion of power among centers in civil society, there was a general expectation that government, good or bad, would necessarily center attention on a single head of state as the primary political decision-maker, perhaps within some constitutional framework. This notion persisted even (one is tempted to say especially) among the revolutionaries. Finally, though the messianic idea had persisted among the immigrants, it was completely secularized and redirected to this-worldly economic and social advancement (individual or collective), even losing the political elements of the older, religiously inspired vision.[13]

Important manifestations of these idea complexes can be seen reflected in the political ideas of subsequent generations of American Jews.[14] Normally quite sophisticated in worldly matters, even those highly attuned to questions of political ideology long retained a curious lack of sophistication in matters of political organization, structure, and polity. In practical terms, this meant that the Jews reacted to the institutions of government, the forces of politics, and the development of issues in ways different from those characteristic of the American people as a whole.

In the beginning, relatively few Jews understood the structure of the American federal system—something which requires a certain amount of political sophistication—and even today relatively few appreciate it on its own terms, although the number is now growing rapidly. Since an understanding of the system has required some sense of local (meaning, in this case, state) involvement as well as national concern, this may be partly accounted for by the Jews' lack of attachment to particular states, even where they have developed ties to certain large cities. More significantly, the immediate past experiences of the Jewish people did not prepare them to appreciate the subtleties of a political system based on the diffusion of power among several centers and placing maximum emphasis on local control.

Jews were used to focusing attention on the single political leader, be he benevolent or malevolent, as the source of all significant political decisions, because in the Old World their communities existed on the sufferance of, and were beholden to, king or emperor.[15] Coming to the United States, they transferred this attention to the president. Thus, *siddurim* published in the United States by Jews of East European ancestry merely substitute a prayer for the president and vice-president while completely ignoring such important elements of American government as the Congress or the states, which, strictly speaking, should receive equal mention in such prayers.[16] Coming to America, they and their descendants have persisted in looking to the national government as the source of all good.

The founders of the United States sought to strengthen the liberties and political rights of all individuals through a system of limited, locally centered government, whose scope of activity was hedged in by a federal system designed to keep power diffused among a number of centers. The pattern is still considered to be the ideal one by most Americans. Even as subsequent generations have modified that pattern in substance, they have sought (with considerable success) to preserve its spirit.[17] The Jews of Europe, on the other hand, found locally centered government, rooted in the communitarian values of the ancient regime, a barrier to their enfranchisement as citizens because it reflected the quasi-feudalism of prerevolutionary days. They supported the French Revolution's assault upon those institutions in the name of collectivism and centralized government, based on Jacobin notions of democratic consent via the "general will" rather than via influence from any local sources.[18]

Government, to most American Jews, long tended to be a matter of law and law-enforcement rather than politics. Nowhere was this more evident until quite recently than in the characteristic channeling of active Jewish political participation through the courts; as a community, American Jewry left its mark on American government in the courtrooms rather than the legislatures or the bureaucracies. The great figures of Jewish origin in American politics tended to be jurists more often than not. Moreover, Jewish organizations with American political missions, particularly the American Jewish Congress, conducted the greater share of their political activities in the courts. While the nature of the issues which interested them was influential in directing them to the courts, the tendency to literalness in viewing the law also led them to reject political solutions, with their built-in demands for compromise based on broad interpretation of the statutes and constitutions.[19] Lying behind these phenomena is a conception of politics-as-law no doubt traceable to the character of Jewish self-government in Europe, where, in common with premodern ideas generally, the notion that men could make positive law through the political process was unknown. Law came from God and Torah, and such changes in the law as were made came from quasi-judicial proceedings, dominated by rabbinical judges who saw themselves as no more than interpreters of the law.[20] Mainstream American notions, on the other hand, have always held law to be a matter of legislation. Even the Constitution, whatever its ultimate connection with "higher law," is a humanly willed document subject to change through the legislative process. Hence, politics is of the essence even under a highly law-oriented system.[21]

Finally, the Jewish immigrants, with their strong penchant for the left, included among their number a considerable leavening of people seeking radical changes in the established order. Unlike most American reformers, they did not start with the view that the political system in which they were located was basically good and that the changes required revolved around a restoration of the proper balance of power within it.[22] (In their European past, the regimes under which they lived had not been basically good.) While the socialists, anarchists, and communists of various shades remained a minority among the immigrants, they did much to set the political tone of the new Jewish communities. They edited the Yiddish periodicals, dominated the speakers' platforms, and organized the first Jewish-dominated political action groups.[23] As part of this interest in radically changing the world, American Jews demonstrated a penchant for messianic internationalism, working for greater American involvement in world affairs at a time when most Americans were isolated. A generation later, American Jews embraced the cause of the United Nations, often seeming to place greater faith in such international organizations than in the representative institutions of the United States.[24]

In several ways, the political notions brought from abroad were strengthened by the experiences of the new immigrants and the political interests generated thereby. The first and foremost political interest of the Jews was to become fully accepted as members of the American body politic.[25] In spite of the bias toward equal acceptance within the American political tradition, the Jews, like other immigrant groups outside the Anglo-Saxon or Nordic cultures, encountered some immediate hostility, usually in the form of social and economic discrimination. Thus the Jews had to engage in a struggle for acceptance; so the Jews, like the others, went left or stayed with the liberals. Then, too, the first direct and continuing contacts between the Jews and government came over questions of church-state relations. At least on the local plane, American governments were concerned with promoting social morality in the biblical spirit, though with an obviously Christian orientation. Sunday "blue laws" designed to "keep the Sabbath holy" seemed to prevent Jews from making a livelihood while observing their Sabbath: public schools where Bible reading and recitation of the Lord's Prayer were common inflicted Christian beliefs on Jewish children; radical prohibitionists among the Protestant fundamentalists threatened the Jewish ceremonial use of wine. In response to these challenges, the Jews adopted a militant separationist position on church-state matters, also akin to that embraced by the European left, and began a battle (which still continues, albeit much-abated and increasingly confined to the last generation's spokesmen) for removal of those "offensive" signs of their minority status.[26] Thus

the Jews were to be found in the paradoxical position of opposing
essentially Jewish ideas as to the religious purposes of civil society in
order to attain equal rights as individuals.

The way in which all these factors made their appearance (or the
way in which the appearance was perceived) tended to persuade
Jews to turn to the federal government for relief, encouraging their
penchant for democracy. While, in actuality, the noncentralized
character of American politics aided the Jews by increasing the value
of their votes in key states, such as New York, Pennsylvania, and
Illinois, the Jews saw national figures—invariably presidents, such
as the two Roosevelts, Wilson, and Truman—as their champions.
They accepted state and local political rewards as their due and
coveted national political recognition; then transferred their sympathies to the national government without appreciating that it was
their local strength that qualified them for consideration in national
councils.[27] Moreover, in church-state questions, the possibility of
successfully appealing to the United States Supreme Court had an
important impact on Jewish attitudes. The court, which had the
additional attraction of being a place where politicking was carried
on through the law in a manner familiar to the Jews, and one which
they were able to master from the start, has responded favorably to
most of the Jews' secularizing demands, thus reinforcing the notion
that federal instrumentalities are more friendly to "democracy" (as
the Jews defined it) and that law is preferable to politics as a means of
gaining democratic goals.

Finally, the fact that most Jews in the United States were first
exposed to local politics in its worst form—in the big cities
dominated by the crudest forms of city bossism—also turned them
toward Washington. The moralistically inclined Jews settled in the
nation's biggest cities when those cities were morally at their nadir.
They were not happy with the ward politics they saw around them,
and, in rejecting them, rejected local government as a democratic
instrument generally.[28]

By holding the ideas they did, the Jews did not stand outside the
broad spectrum of legitimate American political ideas so much as
they stood along its outer limits. In each specific case, they could find

company with other groups safely ensconced within American society, but in no case did they stand close to the mainstream.

With all of the foregoing, the adaptation of the Jews to American politics was quite rapid. That is because in one very important sense, the Jews fitted into the American political pattern immediately. They became attached to reform movements, particularly during the Progressive era, but even earlier their attachment to reform was not so much based on perceptions of self-interest as it was a reflection of the fundamental moral concern which is part and parcel of the Jewish attitude toward politics. Politics, even to the Jews who came to America from an apolitical environment, was considered to be a matter of morality, a device for achieving justice and establishing the good commonwealth. The overwhelming majority of Jewish immigrants could not conceive of politics as a business or a means for personal economic advancement, nor would they accept instructions from any authority or institution (religious or political) as to the casting of their votes. In this respect, the Jews demonstrated from the first that they shared the same political culture as the old-line Yankees, what I have called elsewhere the moralistic political culture.[29] In the United States, this moralistic political culture is one of the nation's three basic political subcultures (the other two being the individualistic and the traditionalistic). These political subcultures reflect differences in political attitudes and outlook that cut across such factors as the date of immigration to American shores, tying together long-established ethnic groups and those more recently arrived with common bonds.[30] The attachment of both the Jews and the heirs of the Puritan tradition to the moralistic political culture is not simply a coincidence. In both cases, the view that politics is a tool to achieve moral ends (rather than simply a means for material advancement or the maintenance of traditional ways of life) comes from the same biblical source. For the Jews, this provided an entree into the American political system at a level appropriate to their interests and background.

Whatever the contradictions between American political ideas and Jewish political notions born out of circumstance, they did not affect the political involvement of the Jews as citizens and voters, perhaps because they did not reflect differences in underlying values. For, despite the apolitical background of the Jewish immigrants to America, no group became involved in the exercise of the rights of American citizens more rapidly than the Jews. The Jews who came to the New World were not peasants like so many of the other immigrants; the great majority were literate and began to follow politics with almost religious zeal because they sensed that political participation was one important way to become Americanized, while it was also good in and of itself in the light of their larger values. As soon as possible, Jews became citizens and voters in the New World, and, having acquired the right to vote, they continued to make use of it in proportions far in excess of the national average and even in excess of the average in comparable socioeconomic groups.[31]

The Jews were involved in politics as progressives or liberals from the first.[32] This, indeed, was true of the earlier Jewish immigrant groups as well. The predominantly Sephardi or Sephardicized Jewish community of the late eighteenth century strongly embraced the American revolutionary cause and then, after the establishment of the United States, became staunch—and in some cases prominent—Jeffersonian Democrats. Jews also followed Andrew Jackson and his persuasion a generation later. Fuchs claims that Jewish ties to the Democratic Party reached their peak in the administration of Martin Van Buren, Jackson's heir to the presidency. The decline of Jewish attachment to that party reflected a general shift of the progressives to the Republican Party. It is very likely that a majority of the German Jews became Republicans from the first. Coming at the time when the struggle over Negro slavery was reaching its peak, their generally anti-slavery sympathies led them into the newly organized GOP.

With the emergence of the conflict over laissez-faire in the last years of the nineteenth century, a majority of the Jews again chose the progressive side. Most of the members of the established Jewish community sympathized with the progressives, even if they stood on the right wing of the reform movement. Among the new immigrants there were many socialists who attempted, at first, to transfer their

Old World ideas to the American scene. In time, most of them became supporters of Franklin D. Roosevelt, the New Deal, and the Democratic Party. The bulk of the new immigrants ultimately arrived at the same position, though not via socialism. As early as 1900, the Jews of New York City voted solidly for William Jennings Bryan, the Democratic candidate for president, despite his associations with the supposed nativism of the greater West, which years later led certain historians of Jewish birth to denigrate his credentials as a progressive. The next year, the Jewish voters of that city were instrumental in electing a reform administration, joining with the uptown "blue bloods" in a fusion movement.[33]

From the 1890s until the early 1930s, when both the Democratic and the Republican parties contained active conservative and progressive or liberal wings which struggled within each party for control, the Jews voted independently, choosing candidates for their personal stands rather than following one party or the other consistently. Thus the Jewish vote went for both Bryan, the Democrat, and Theodore Roosevelt, the Republican, on the basis of their progressivism without regard to their party differences. As the progressive-liberal coalition won greater power in the Democratic Party and the conservatives increased their hold on the GOP, the Jews moved toward the former.[34]

By the 1930s, American Jews had given their full commitment to the Democratic Party, which not only offered a prospective solution to the problems of the depression, but also offered Eastern European Jews the kind of political recognition previously accorded only to Sephardi and German Jews.[35] This commitment to the Democratic Party has persisted, but less today for manifestly ethnic reasons and more for reasons of ideology. The Jews of the 1970s vote Democratic because they are liberals in the way their fathers voted Democratic because they were Jewish.[36] Nevertheless, the latest association clearly remains.

In any case, the commitment of the Jewish voters to liberal candidates and causes has been consistent and overwhelming. Such statistics on the matter as are available show that from 65 to over 90 percent of the Jewish voters have supported the Democratic ticket in national elections since the New Deal. And, in every case, this support has included Jews from economic levels that among non-Jews have continued to vote Republican.[37]

Whatever their early difficulties, the Jews in the United States have had unparallelled success in expressing their basic sociopolitical instincts as a function of their securing full membership in a predominantly non-Jewish society. The facts of that success are well-known and need not be documented here. The reasons for that success are somewhat more conjectural, but even they are reasonably familiar. I would suggest that three reasons of first importance should be accepted, at least one of which is directly related to the points made in the previous section.

1. American society has traditionally been an open society that has valued some measure of pluralism from the first, and it came into being with no established feudal institutions to militate against full integration of non-Christians into the "American way of life."

2. America has had a dynamic society with a continually growing economy offering new opportunities in every generation. The nation has never been forced to redivide the same economic pie, but has been able to give new groups a share in an economy that is ever-expanding. Moreover, those (like the Jews) who have been able to contribute significantly to the nation's growth, have been especially welcome to share in the growing economic pie.

3. The basic values, both positive and negative, of the American and Jewish civilizations are quite similar, encouraging a measure of convergence and identification not present in other civilizations that have been hosts to Jews.

Successful Jewish integration into American society has been coupled with great successes in the economic and intellectual realms. In the former, the Jews as a group have achieved the highest level of material prosperity of any single ethnic group in the country, while at the same time making important contributions to the American economy as a whole. In the latter realm, individual Jews have, in recent years, become the nation's pace-setters.

In politics and governmental service, however, the Jewish record was distinctly mixed. In the political realm, at least a few Jews participated as individuals everywhere, holding every office except the very highest in the land. (Today even that office is no longer considered unattainable.) Yet, unlike members of other immigrant groups, such as the Irish and Italians, few Jews sought to advance themselves through politics, preferring to follow business, professional, and intellectual pursuits for economic and social advancement. Thus, despite a measure of Jewish activity in numbers out of proportion to their 3 percent or less of the total population, Jews were not nearly as visible in public life as in other fields. Take, for example, the employment pattern of Jews in Detroit in 1935. Less than 1 percent of the gainfully occupied Jews in that city were engaged in the public services. Whereas the Jews constituted 5.9 percent of the gainfully employed in all industries, they constituted only 1.7 percent of those in the public service—less, if women are excluded.[38] In a survey of 234 cities, conducted between 1948 and 1951, John P. Dean found that "the participation of Jews in politics or in public office appears to be relatively limited, compared for instance, with that of Irish, Italian or other immigrant descended groups"; that "participation is somewhat greater in appointive office . . ."; and that "the most common type is the appointment of lawyers to positions such as assistant district attorney, civil service commissioner, or housing commissioner."[39]

Until very recently, even those Jews who later became political leaders all entered public life after having made careers elsewhere. Moreover, the Jews of the last migration and their descendants have been distinctly underrepresented as a group among those Jews who have been leaders in political affairs. The Sephardi Jews, with their prior background in Western societies (even though they never constituted more than a few thousand souls), produced numerous men who entered public affairs as early as the seventeenth century; and they continued to do so for three centuries. The German Jews, within one generation of their arrival in significant numbers, contributed political figures who were able to compete in national politics. Eastern European Jewry only began to produce men of recognized importance after three generations.[40]

The Jews expressed their political concern in other ways, however, primarily through voluntary service in the cause of radicalism or reform. In the early years, this involved activity in specialized or fringe organizations. Then Jews became active as amateurs or volunteers in mainstream political groups, with increasing success in recent years. This volunteering spirit persists today, most recently in the civil rights movement in the South, where the number of Jews may have exceeded 50 percent of the white participants, and the Peace Corps, where, in its heyday, the Jews were reported to have composed some 60 percent of the volunteers.[41]

A decade ago, the foregoing analysis could have stopped at this point. Since the mid-1960s, however, there have been notable changes in the pattern of American Jewish political participation. In the first place, relatively large numbers of individual *Jews* become visibly active in the political arena—as office holders and candidates, campaign and party activists, and as major financial contributors, Jews began to emerge in even more significant numbers in the highest appointive positions in the federal, state, and local governments. Shortly thereafter, Jews began to openly pursue collective Jewish interests in the political arena. These two developments marked a semi-drainage in the relationship of America's Jews to American politics.

Perhaps it was the Kennedy breakthrough in 1960 which signaled to the white non-Protestant minorities in America that politics was now open to them even outside their neighborhoods. I believe that JFK's victory in the presidential election of that year was more a symptom than a cause, a reflection of the advancing of America's "two cities." From the late nineteenth century until after World War II, the country was divided into "two cities," which enabled the white Protestant majority in the upper city to dominate "prestige politics," while the "ethnics" and the Jews could play their role almost exclusively in areas where they were concentrated, and non-whites were essentially excluded from playing any political role at all. The two cities began to merge into one after World War II, and the process was much accelerated during the 1960's to the point where I believe it is fair to say that they have now merged, at least in the political realm. The merger was accomplished by those who entered politics through the Democratic Party in the wake of the Kennedy campaign and through the Republican Party in the wake of the Goldwater campaign four years later. Among them were many Jews.

One result of all this was that Jews began to run for the more visible offices—at one time, a few years back, there were Jewish governors or U. S. senators holding office simultaneously in Rhode Island, Connecticut, New York, Pennsylvania, Ohio, and Maryland —the bloc of states forming the heart of the Northeast, America's "main street." Another result was that the presence of Jews in political campaigns and party affairs became far more pronounced and visible, up to Democratic National Committee chairman. And the role of Jews as contributors to candidates of both parties has become a matter of well-discussed public record. This trend not only reflected greater ease of access to the political arena, but also a new understanding of and empathy with American politics on the part of the third and fourth generations of American Jews, whose roots were "all American" in a certain real sense. Virtually all of these Jewish political activists entered politics for personal reasons as Americans, pure and simple (the few exceptions, if any, may be found among the contributors of funds). They did not seek to express any Jewish interests, per se. But the events of the late 1960s—the increased militancy of blacks, often directed against Jews for a variety of reasons; the 1967 Arab-Israel war and its aftermath of Israeli dependence upon the United States (especially after the Yom Kippur War); the opening of a new stage in the civil rights revolution, calling for "affirmative action" and quotas under whatever guise—caused many Jews to perceive that they had certain political concerns as Jews, and, in their newfound political "savvy" and involvement, they could see their way clear to expressing their collective interests in the political arena. In the 1970s, they began to organize to do so in a variety of ways—in some cases extending the previous organizational efforts and in some cases developing new ones. In certain cases, their efforts became identifiably and visibly Jewish.

It remains to be seen whether or not this emergence of highly visible Jewish political involvement is a transitional phenomenon. Historically Jews have risen to high office or otherwise became visibly politically in periods of transition when the power systems of the countries in which they were located were undergoing change. Is America different? There is no way to predict the future in this matter.

Looking at the evolving relationship between the political notions of the American Jews and American political ideas generally, there has been a general tendency for the bulk of American Jews gradually to Americanize their political notions, but with an interesting and important cleavage in their manner of doing so. The general Jewish population has done so uncritically, simply as part of their overall assimilation into American life. Certain Jewish intellectuals, on the other hand, have either fought that Americanization or have sought to alter American political ideas themselves.

The Americanization of Jews came about at a time when there was a leftward shift in the political notions of the American majority as well, as a result of the pressure of twentieth-century war, depression, and technology. Simultaneously, as Jews were developing political savvy, more of the crucial decisions confronting Americans were being transferred to the courts. As a result, a certain convergence has taken place between the United States and its laws. While American Jews today more than ever before resemble the American majority in their overt political behavior, the Jews reached their present political position by turning from an even more leftist one (either socialist or strongly inclined toward the left), while the American majority has turned toward an acceptance of the welfare state, with considerable reluctance, from an earlier limited or anti-government position. The difference in their respective directions of evolution reflects a difference in immediate political ideas and is also a reflection of different social experiences.

Despite the uniqueness of the Jewish experience in America, one sees marked similarities between their support of the liberal left (or left-liberals) and the general tendency of Jews the world over to support the same groups in their respective countries since the French Revolution. These common attitudes appeared and were grounded in the Jews' immediate political experiences all over the Western world in the century following emancipation. To the extent that the liberal-left has been an agent for the achievement of greater social justice, these favorable attitudes have been reinforced by

Jewish tradition (there is some evidence that this reinforcement was direct wherever the two streams came into contact); but the simple sociological fact of Jewish interest in emancipation and equal rights, and the promotion of that interest by the left, is sufficient to explain this leaning afterward by a people noted in other respects for its conservatism.

What of the relationship between contemporary Jewish political ideas and classical Jewish political thought? I believe that there is such a thing as classical Jewish political thought, even though, in the course of so many centuries of absence from political life in the normal sense, the Jews have virtually forgotten its existence even when it speaks out to them from the pages of their sacred texts, particularly the Bible and the Talmud. The contents of classical Jewish political thought cannot be set forth in any detail here. Basically, the political thought of the sacred texts looks to two things: (1) government by and through a covenant system, and (2) politics as a form of moral action. From the first flow several principles of political organization, and from the second, several principles of political purpose, all of which (and their various applications) were discussed, either directly or through illustration, in the Bible and the Talmud. Using the terminology of today's political science, we may say that the first leads to ideas of constitutionalism, limited and republican government, and dispersal of power among different centers (both public and private) in a manner reminiscent of federalism or derivatives of the federal principle. The second leads to notions of the activist state, with overtones of public regulation of individual enterprise on behalf of the common good and for the protection of individuals as well. A summary of the prophetic vision of the ideal commonwealth as presented in the book of Joshua reveals all of this clearly. There, in the course of an idealized description of the Israelite conquest of Canaan, the author presents a vision of a tribal federation (1) operating under a Divine constitution with (2) a national government led by (3) a strong charismatic leader who is the servant of God (not sovereign in his own right) and is thus bound by the constitution to obey its terms and to consult with (4) the national assembly, which is representative of the tribes, and embracing (5) tribal and local governments structured along republican lines, each man under his own vine and fig tree, where his rights are protected by law, and in which he joins with the authorities to protect the rights of his neighbors.[42]

Reading the statement presented here in its simplicity, we might conclude that classical Jewish political thought is virtually identical with the American political tradition. Though, in a broad sense, there are clear similarities, there are certain points of equally clear contradiction between the two, and there are others in which unresolved problems could indicate potential points of disagreement. Classical Jewish political thought, for example, starts from the premise that the truth is given to man by God and that properly qualified authorities must protect the truth by suppressing certain kinds of error. There is certainly an element containing this view within the American political tradition, but American liberalism does not accept it, and the liberal view has been dominant. On another level, the American notion that every man is free to choose his religion and his citizenship cannot easily be squared with the Jewish notion of national and religious inheritance. Of course, there are also great differences in the level of sophistication of the political institutions developed out of the two systems.

Nevertheless, the convergence between the two systems is remarkable, especially if we consider the great gulf in time and space that separates their points of origin. This convergence can be explained historically, but for our purposes here it is sufficient to recognize its existence, particularly in the light of the considerable contradiction between the political notions brought to America by the Jews and the ideas of the American political tradition.

Today, American Jews are edging away from the political notions of their immediate ancestors. In some cases the change is almost a caricature of assimilation, as when Jews in Texas become supporters of the radical right like their non-Jewish neighbors, and Jewish doctors back the most conservative Republicans because they fear the possibility of socialized medicine, or, conversely, when Jewish intellectuals advocate legalization of various abnormal sexual practices in the name of liberalism and freedom. In most cases, however, the change is one of newly found interest in and commitment to a political tradition now unreservedly theirs.

The decline of the issues of the French Revolution in contemporary politics has given most American Jews a chance to relate to the very different political ideals of America. Curiously enough, in doing this, they may be returning—albeit unaware—to political ideas more closely related to those endorsed in the classical Jewish sources (the Bible and the Talmud), such as federalism, communitarianism, and republican government within a democratic context—the very ideas which the Americans initially derived in large measure from the Bible.

NOTES

1. A good general summary of the political concerns of Jews from the mid-sixteenth to the mid-twentieth century can be found in Howard M. Sachar, *The Course of Modern Jewish History* (New York, 1958).

Unless otherwise indicated, the American Jews referred to in this article are those who have come to the United States since 1881 from Eastern Europe, and their descendants. The Jews of this group form the bulk (well over 80 percent) of the American Jewish community. Consequently, their attitudes dominate American Jewish life. This is not to minimize the degree to which the earlier waves of Jewish immigration (the Sephardi–Western European and German–Central European elements) and their descendants have shared the same ideas or contributed to American Jewish life. In fact, the most notable Jewish contributions to American public affairs have been made by the descendants of those earlier waves, but with few exceptions, the contributions were made by individuals, whose impact on the ideas of American Jewry came as a consequence of their public recognition, but who themselves reflected ideas acquired from a predominantly non-Jewish environment. There will be specific reference to these earlier immigrants where their influence has been relevant.

Furthermore, because of space limitations, the discussion of American Jewish political notions is couched in the most general terms. No significant effort is made to draw lines of distinction between the notions of different Jews or Jewish groups. The discussion of American political ideas is similarly couched in the most general terms. Unless qualified, the reference to "American political ideas" is invariably to the classic ideas of the American political tradition, formulated and expressed in the first century of American independence. Twentieth-century modifications of these ideas are specified within the body of the paper where necessary.

2. See Ralph Henry Gabriel, *The Course of American Democratic Thought* (New York, 1940), and David W. Minar, *Ideas and Politics: The American Experience* (Homewood, Ill., 1964).

3. Discussions of the influence of biblical ideas, with particular reference to England, can be found in Edwyn R. Bevan and Charles Singer, eds., *The Legacy of Israel* (London, 1927), particularly the essays by Smith, Box, Isaacs, Selbie, and Roth. For their influence in the United States, see Joseph Gaer and Ben Siegel, *The Puritan Heritage: America's Roots in the Bible* (New York, 1964); Perry Miller, *The New England Mind* (New York, 1939), particularly "The Seventeenth Century"; and Oscar S. Straus, *The Origin of the Republican Form of Government in the United States of America* (New York, 1926).

4. For a discussion of this, see Daniel Boorstin, *The Genius of American Politics* (Chicago, 1953).

5. For a discussion of agrarianism as a persistent influence in the United States, see Henry Bamford Parkes, *The American Experience* (New York, 1947), and Anselm Strauss, *Images of the American City* (New York, 1961), especially chap. 10

6. See *International Encyclopedia of the Social Sciences*, "s.v. Federalsim."

7. See, for example, David Noble, *Historians Against History* (Minneapolis, 1965).

8. For a survey of the biblical discussion of these four elements, see John Bright, *A History of Israel* (Philadelphia, 1959), particularly chap. 4. See also Yehezkel

Kaufmann's discussion of the political ideas of ancient Israel in *The Religion of Israel* (Chicago, 1962).

9. See Ruth Miller Elson, *Guardians of Tradition: American Schoolbooks of the Nineteenth Century* (Lincoln, Nebr. 1964), for a biased but thorough account of the contents of the school texts. By the same token, the politicization of the Jews, once they came to the United States, led them to begin to see the political elements in the Bible. See, for example, *Jewish Tidings*, December 14, 1886, for an explicit reference in this regard.

10. Salo W. Baron, *The Jewish Community* (Philadelphia, 1942), particularly vol. 2.

11. Sachar, op. cit., and Ismar Elbogen, *A Century of Jewish Life* (Philadelphia, 1944), provide the best discussions of the overall Jewish movement to the liberal left. While studies of Jewish voting behavior in Europe are few, those that exist confirm this. See, for example, Walter B. Simon, "The Jewish Vote in Vienna," *Jewish Social Studies* 23, no. 1 (January 1961).

12. See Sachar, op. cit., chapter 16; Lawrence H. Fuchs, *The Political Behavior of American Jews* (Glencoe, Ill., 1956); Werner Cohn, "Sources of American Jewish Liberalism: A Study of the Political Alignments of American Jews" (Ph.D. diss., New School for Social Research, 1956); Charles S. Liebman, *The Ambivalent American Jew* (Philadelphia, 1971); and Milton Himmelfarb, *The Jews of Modernity* (New York, 1973).

13. See Baron, op. cit.; Sachar, op. cit.; Elbogen, op. cit., particularly chaps. 5, 6, 13, and 14, for a survey of the development and functioning of these idea complexes, particularly in European Jewry. Ben Halpern presents a discussion of the ideological roots of American Jewish attitudes to Judaism in *The American Jew: A Zionist Analysis* (New York, 1956). See Himmelfarb, op. cit., and Hebman, op. cit.

14. Unfortunately, research to this effect is hard to come by. The sense of the situation becomes apparent, however, when one examines the standard sociological studies of American Jewry. See, for example, Marshall Sklare, ed., *The Jews: Social Patterns of an American Group* (Glencoe, Ill., 1958). Perhaps more impressive is the pattern of Jewish historical writing. Focusing on either national or community histories, only the Jews of the trans-Mississippi West, as a rule, have produced histories of the Jews of particular states.

15. See Baron, op. cit.; Heinrich Graetz, *History of the Jews* (Philadelphia, 1891), vols. 3, 4, and 5; or any specialized history of the Jewish communities of medieval Europe, for discussions of this relationship.

16. This is true even in such Americanized *siddurim* as that of the United Synagogue. Contrast the American Sephardi *siddur*, which refers to "the President and Vice President of the United States of America, the Governor, the Lieutenant Governor, and the people of this State represented in Senate and Assembly, and the magistrates of this city." David de Sola Pool, ed. and trans., *Book of Prayer According to the Custom of the Spanish and Portuguese Jews* (New York: Union of Sephardic Congregations, 1941), p. 204.

17. William Anderson discusses this in *The Nation and the States: Rivals or Partners?* (Minneapolis, 1955).

18. Cohn, op. cit., discusses the antipathy between the Jews and locally centered political authority.

19. See, for example, the publications of the American Jewish Congress regarding civil rights legislation and court action.

20. See Louis Finkelstein, *Jewish Self-Government in the Middle Ages*, 2d ed. (New York, 1964).

21. See, for example, Herbert Agar, *The Price of Union* (Boston, 1950).

22. The Jewish attitude is discussed in Abraham Menes, "The Jewish Labor Movement," in *The Jewish People, Past and Present* (New York: YIVO, 1955), vol. 4. The American attitude is exemplified in Russel B. Nye, *Midwestern Progressive Politics* (East Lansing, Mich., 1951).

23. Menes, op. cit., and Sachar, op. cit., chap. 16.

24. Lawrence H. Fuchs, "Sources of Jewish Internationalism and Liberalism," in Sklare, op. cit., pp. 595–613.

25. Anita Libman Lebeson, *Pilgrim People* (New York, 1950), presents a standard view of this overriding purpose and the accepted chronicle of how it was achieved.

26. The so-called defense organizations, beginning with the American Jewish Committee and including the Anti-Defamation League and the American Jewish Congress, have all adopted this posture despite the differences among them on other issues that are judged from the "conservative-liberal" perspective. The chronicle of their efforts is available in the *American Jewish Year Book*, published annually by the Jewish Publication Society since 1899 and the American Jewish Committee.

27. Despite the attention they gave their radicals, the Jews did gain power politically when they used their "muscle" as voters in particular states and localities. Thus the Jews of New York's East Side took a major step forward when they elected Meyer London to represent them in Congress in 1914 (Sachar, op. cit., pp. 324–25). It has been suggested that even the great Brandeis achieved national office only after he developed roots in the Jewish community, and thus filled the political requirements which President Wilson had to accept; cf. Yonathan Shapiro, "American Jews in Politics: The Case of Louis D. Brandeis," *American Jewish Historical Quarterly* 60, no. 2 (December 1965).

28. Nathan Glazer and Daniel Patrick Moynihan discuss this in the case of the largest Jewish community in the United States, in *Beyond the Melting Pot* (Cambridge, Mass., 1963), pp. 137–80. See Charles Bernheimer, ed., *The Russian Jew in the United States* (New York: Young People's Missionary Movement, 1905), for a contemporary discussion of East European Jewish political experiences in the Old World and involvements in the New.

29. Daniel J. Elazar, *American Federalism: A View From the States* (New York, 1966), chap. 4.

30. Briefly, the moralistic political culture views politics primarily as a means to advance the public good; the individualistic political culture accepts politics as a means for individuals to advance themselves economically and socially; and the traditionalistic political culture views politics primarily as a means to support an established social order.

31. Bernheimer, op. cit.; Fuchs, op. cit.; Glazer and Moynihan, op. cit.; and Sachar, op. cit. See also Stuart E. Rosenberg, "Notes on the Political Attitudes of the *Jewish Tidings*," *Jewish Social Studies* 17, no. 4 (October 1955).

32. The following paragraphs are based on Cohn, op. cit.; Fuchs, op. cit.; and Lebeson, op. cit.

33. Bernheimer, op. cit., pp. 256–79.

34. Until the New Deal, the Orthodox Yiddish press was generally Republican, partly in opposition to the dominant Jewish socialists of the Lower East Side, and partly as a reflection of their predilection for conservatism in politics as well as religion. The German Jews were also predominantly Republicans in this period; see Cohn, op. cit.

35. The New Deal also brought the Jewish socialists into the Democratic ranks. See Cohn, op. cit., and Bernard D. Weinryb, "The Adaptation of Jewish Labor Groups to American Life," *Jewish Social Studies* 7, no. 4 (October 1946).

36. Recent studies to this effect include Maurice G. Guysenir, "Jewish Vote in Chicago," *Jewish Social Studies*, 20, no. 4 (October 1958), and Edgar Litt, "Status, Ethnicity, and Patterns of Jewish Voting Behavior in Baltimore," *Jewish Social Studies* 22, no. 3 (July 1960).

37. This is not to say that there is absolutely no correlation between economic level and voting behavior among American Jews. Among those Jews whose earnings are in the upper 10 percent, there appears to be a clear tendency for nearly a majority of them to vote Republican. See Judith R. Kramer and Seymour Leventman, *Children of the Gilded Ghetto* (New Haven, 1961), which indicates that this was the case for the Jews in Minneapolis in the 1956 presidential election. It has proven even more true.

38. Henry J. Meyer, "The Economic Structure of the Jewish Community in Detroit," *Jewish Social Studies* 2, no. 2 (April 1940).

39. John P. Dean, "Patterns of Socialization and Association Between Jews and Non-Jews," *Jewish Social Studies* 17, no. 3 (July 1955).

40. While no overall calculations are available for the nation as a whole, a survey of the names associated with political affairs in the standard histories of American Jewry will confirm this observation. See, for example, the names cited in Lebeson, op. cit. For more specific examples, see the names listed in Louis J. Swichkow and Lloyd P. Gartner, *The History of the Jews of Milwaukee* (Philadelphia, 1963), app. 32, "Milwaukee Jews Who Held Public Office," pp. 514–18. In the necrology lists of the *American Jewish Year Book*, vols. 62–66, covering the period from July 1, 1959 to December 3, 1964, twenty-six Jews are listed as having held public office, appointive or elective. One was of Sephardi origin, seven of Eastern European birth or parentage, and eighteen were descended from German Jews.

41. The author received this information from confidential sources.

42. Yehezkel Kaufmann makes a case for the classical character of premonarchical political ideas in the Jewish tradition. See, for example, his chapter, "Israel in Canaan," in Leo W. Schwarz, ed., *Great Ages and Ideas of the Jewish People* (New York, 1956), particularly pp. 38–53. See also the sources cited in n. 6 above for further discussion of these ideas and their classical character.

SELECTED BIBLIOGRAPHY

Fuchs, Lawrence H. *The Political Behavior of American Jews*. Glencoe, Ill.; Free Press, 1956.

Glazer, Nathan, and Moynihan, Daniel P. *Beyond the Melting Pot*. Cambridge, Mass., M.I.T. Press, 1963.

Himmelfarb, Milton. *The Jews of Modernity.* New York, Basic Books, 1973.

Isaacs, Stephen D. *Jews and American Politics.* Garden City, N. Y., Doubleday, 1974.

Porter, Jack N., and Dreier, Peter, eds. *Jewish Radicalism: A Selected Anthology.* New York, Grove Press, 1973.

Rosenstock, Morton. *Louis Marshall: Defender of Jewish Rights.* Detroit: Wayne State University Press, 1965.

Sklare, Marshall, ed. *The Jews: Social Patterns of an American Group.* Glencoe, Ill.: Free Press, 1958.

The Future of the Jewish Community in America: A Perspective and Agenda

DAVID SIDORSKY

THERE IS A MEASURE of irony in the constant appeal to historians and social scientists to predict or to project the future of the society that they study. For if there is any single conclusion that emerges from the study of history and of the social sciences, it would seem to be that the historical or social process is unpredictable.

This conclusion does not deny, of course, that historians have written plausible accounts of how present events have developed from the preceding situation. There are many important historical works that have given us a better understanding of a society by exhibiting how historical persons with particular kinds of motivations and sets of abilities have participated in the transformation of social situations.

Similarly, this conclusion of historical unpredictability does not contradict the success of the social sciences. Economists, demographers, and sociologists have selected complex data and isolated crucial variables, and then provided illuminating correlations with other important data. Illustrations abound, from the significance of the expansion of the supply of money for the rate of price inflation to the relevance of the population mix in a particular geographical area for the rate of interreligious marriage in that area.

The point remains that these achievements, whether of historians or of social scientists, fall far short of an ability to predict the future character of a community or society.

It is a speculative task, engendering great controversy, to inquire into an explanation of this unpredictability. Some have pointed to the complexity of the historical process, in which there is an intersection of variables studied in different sciences, from seismology to psychology, as the reason for this unpredictability. Others have stressed the role of human decision and choice in the determination of an open historical future. Still others have looked for an explanation in the distinction between lawlike correlations of a statistical sort among groups of events, which have been attained by the social or physical scientist, and the forecast of the detailed career of a single entity or historical agent, which has not been attained. Whatever be the merits of these and other contending or overlapping accounts of the reasons for the unpredictability of history, both common sense and the study of the record of past historical predictions confirm the fact.

Consequently, despite the title of this lecture, I am not concerned with the prediction or projection of the future. My focus is upon achieving a perspective of the present condition of the Jewish community and of some of the choices that currently confront the members of that community.

One obvious starting point for such a perspective is to take note of the fact that the American Jewish community is today one of the three major centers of population of Jewish people. Of the more than twelve million Jews in the world, slightly less than half live in the United States of America. About one quarter of that population live in Israel, and nearly that many are estimated to live in the Soviet Union. One of the fundamental areas of choice for the American Jewish community, both in its organized institutional framework and in individual activities, is the patterning of its relationships with the Jewish communities of Israel and the Soviet Union. There is an element of historical drama in the patterning of those relationships, since the three communities represent the carrying out, so to speak, of the ideological options for the Jewish people advanced in the nineteenth century. That history impinges upon the decisions that will govern the future relationships among those three communities, and it merits, therefore, a measure of explanation.

The American Jewish Community in Historical Perspective

The ideology of the Jewish emancipation in Europe in the nineteenth century projected a historical future in which the Jewish communities (first of the Western European countries and subsequently of the Eastern European countries as well) would successfully overcome the disabilities of their status as an alien, segregated, and persecuted group. The proponents of emancipation asserted, both as a moral ideal and as a realizable historical option, the possibility of a radical transformation of the unsatisfactory Jewish condition. This transformation involved elements of political, social, and religious change in the environment in which Jews found themselves at that time.

Politically, they looked forward to a society which would guarantee civil liberties for all individuals, regardless of their religious or ethnic affiliation. On their view, such a society required the political enactment of a separation of church and state so that religious affiliation would be irrelevant in contexts of public affairs. This separation would be accompanied by the general establishment of the principle of equality before the law and of a high degree of political tolerance and political pluralism.

Socially, the emancipation of the Jews, or of other minorities, was to bring about their participation in all aspects of the new secular culture. In Europe after the Enlightenment, this presented a horizon of great possibilities in science, the arts, education, and even the media of entertainment.

Religiously, the emancipation involved a movement of accommodation of Judaism to modernity and to the demands of the modern, secular, nation-state. Specifically, there emerged within the first half of the nineteenth century three trends in Jewish religion, each of which accomplished a distinctive pattern of accommodation. First, the Reform movement introduced minor adjustments in Jewish rituals so as to make them seemingly more compatible with Western cultural styles. More controversially, it also undertook to eliminate those aspects of the ethnic or rabbinic traditions of Judaism which it believed to be inappropriate for contemporary enlightened religious belief or practice. Second, the Neo-Orthodox movement adumbrated an Orthodox Jewish pattern of observance which could be carried out within the new milieus in which Jews found themselves outside of the segregated Jewish community. Third, the Conservative movement argued for the retention of the historic traditions of

Judaism while accepting many changes in Jewish observance, presumably as requisite for adjustment to the new European environment. In consequence, the once fixed pattern of Jewish religious observance was now augmented by three additional modes of Jewish religious membership. Further, the patterns of voluntary association which characterize modern, secular society meant that Jewish affiliation could be carried on by membership in Jewish communal or fraternal organizations in which religious belief or observance was ignored.

By the second half of the nineteenth century, when Jewish immigration from Europe to the United States began to assume significant dimensions, the emancipation had recast many of the major features of the European Jewish community.

There were two main ideological tendencies within European Jewish life and thought that rejected the theses of the supporters of Jewish emancipation. The socialist claim, argued by the young Karl Marx in the first disappointing phase of Jewish emancipation in Germany, and by several subsequent generations of socialist thinkers, was that the ideal of Jewish emancipation was undesirable, and more important, unachievable under the conditions of bourgeois society. The socialists argued that capitalist society granted "formal freedom," that is, legal rights to all citizens who were excluded from power, but it would never bring them a measure of "concrete freedom," that is, equality of participation and power in the economic, social, and political life of the society. The realization of the ideal of freedom or equality for all citizens of the modern state, in their view, could only come about with the revolutionary transformation of nationalist, Christian, capitalist culture. Accordingly, any promise of emancipation for the Jews would be an illusion until after the socialist revolution. This revolution, on the Marxist account, would require the withering away of both religion and nationality so that the emancipated citizens would all share a common universal, humanist, and socialist culture.

Within the Jewish socialist movement of the nineteenth century, which gained a large following among the masses of poor Jews in the Eastern European cities and among the secular intelligentsia, the Marxist doctrine was systematically reinterpreted. That reinterpretation provided for a socialist cultural and political movement which would express its socialist ideals in the particular forms and idioms of its national linguistic heritage. The secular Yiddish socialist movement looked forward to such a form of Jewish emancipation: autonomous cultural rights for the Jewish community within a socialist state framework. The abolition of anti-Semitism after the Russian Revolution led some to believe that this kind of emancipation might take place in the Soviet Union, despite restrictions on individual freedom of religion, right of emigration, and diversity of expression.

The other ideological tendency which rejected the possibility of Jewish emancipation was Zionism. There were diverse roots for the Zionist movement and many different kinds of expression of this skepticism about the feasibility of Jewish emancipation in Europe. These diverse opinions have continued to shape the perspectives within which the possibilities of the Jewish community are surveyed. Theodor Herzl, the founder of political Zionism, believed that the emancipation of the Jews of Europe was illusory since anti-Semitism survived like a dormant volcano which might erupt and engulf the entire Jewish population. The Dreyfus case in France was, for Herzl, a dramatic illustration of the latent survival of anti-Semitism in Western Europe a full century after the initial grant of civil liberties to the French Jewish community. Moses Hess, the founder of socialist Zionism, argued that even under socialism, the passion of nationalist prejudice would not wither away, so that radical transformation of society would be compatible with a continuity of anti-Semitism in the new egalitarian framework. Ahad Ha'am, the founder of cultural Zionism, suggested that Jewish emancipation in the countries of Western Europe was fraudulent. It offered the Jews freedom, but tacitly exacted the price of a denial of spiritual identity for the right to exercise that freedom. Accordingly, he considered the emancipation a form of servitude in the guise of freedom which Jews should reject out of national self-respect.

The sharpness of the confrontation between Zionist ideology and the more prevalent pro-emancipation attitudes can be judged from the Zionist assertion that it represented a movement for "auto-emancipation." The only road to full civil or political rights for the

Jewish community, in the Zionist view, was not to strive for equality of legal rights for the individual Jew within the European sovereign state, but to achieve freedom for the national group through a sovereign Jewish state. In such a state, Jews would have political equality as a matter of course. More important, they would have achieved freedom or self-determination of their cultural and religious life as a community as well.

There was an additional element of Zionist ideology which plays a part in current relationships among the Jewish communities of Israel, America, and Russia. The Zionist thesis was that the existence of a sovereign Jewish state would normalize the condition of Jewish existence throughout the world. According to that thesis, anti-Semitism was caused by the alien, pariah, abnormal status of the Jews within Diaspora societies as well as by the vulnerability of the Jew as an alien in those societies. Once the Jews living in the Diaspora were viewed as people connected with their own nation-state, like any other ethnic or religious minority within a pluralistic society, the image of their abnormality would change. On the view of many Zionists, the result of that process would be the withering away of anti-Semitism. The claims of the Zionist ideology were formulated in both minimal and maximal variants. The minimal claim was that a sovereign Jewish state would provide a refuge for potential victims of anti-Semitism who would need a territory for refuge. The more optimistic hope was that within a Jewish state, there would be a renaissance of civic spirit and national culture which would reshape the future of the Jewish community throughout the world.

The history of Zionist settlement in Palestine and of the founding and development of the State of Israel cannot be read as a realization of the ideological projection of Zionism. Yet the patterns of Zionist faith have been of critical importance for that history.

The American Jewish Community in Relationship to Soviet Jewry and to Israel

With the preceding sketch of the three ideological tendencies of Jewry in the nineteenth century—emancipation, socialism, Zionism—it is instructive to examine the relationship among the three communities, each of which represents in a significant manner elements of realization of a different tendency: the United States as a post-emancipation community, Israel as the post-Zionist community, and the Soviet Union as the post-socialist community.

It is not our purpose here to relate the history of the Soviet Jewish community except as it currently affects the Jewish community of the United States. The tragic ways in which totalitarianism undermined any basis for humanist socialist culture and for secular Yiddish cultural expression in the Soviet Union have influenced the direction of Jewish expression in the United States. The Soviet experience was one of several factors contributing to the virtual demise of the movement for secular Yiddish culture in the United States. This in turn influenced the development of Jewish community organization in the United States, particularly after the Second World War, toward the direction of congregational, religious patterns of affiliation rather than secular, ethnic associations. To the degree to which American Jewish culture has always faced toward external models, the condition of Soviet Jewry, like the destruction of European Jewry, has brought about a situation in which the community faces primarily toward Israel.

There can be no doubt that the more recent developments within the Soviet Jewish community have also had an impact on the condition of the American Jewish community, although it is difficult to assess that impact. The assertion of Jewish identity by a significant segment of Russian Jews, fifty years after the revolution and in the face of repression and terror, has generated a response among many circles within the American Jewish community. Two aspects of that response seem particularly significant. First, it has involved a shift in the moral perceptions of many members of the Jewish community from the support of moral ideals that are linked to universalist values toward support of the particular rights of Jews to assert their Jewish identity or to emigrate to Israel. Such a shift in perception affects the general terms of the perennial debate within the Jewish community on the degree to which communal efforts should be directed to the fulfillment of shared universal ideals or to the specific support of Jewish interests or rights.

Second, the communal agenda of the Jewish community had often been defined, in its public policy aspects, in defensive or philanthropic terms. The defensive part of the agenda involved group-relations activities against anti-Semitism; the philanthropic part of the agenda involved a network of hospitals and social-service agencies. Other aspects of Jewish communal activities, including support for Jewish education and for Israel, were viewed as expressions of particular religious or Zionist groups, not as part of public policy. The introduction of support for the rights of Soviet Jews to emigrate to Israel as part of the public policy agenda, like the simultaneous growth of support of Israel, marked a new activism within Jewish communal activity. Such an activism could energize secular ethnic groups as well as traditional religious groups in activities that were challenging and gratifying. So the involvement of the Jewish community in the United States in support of the rights of Soviet Jews had an important fall-out in the internal Jewish morale of the community. How pervasive, deep, or continuous that impact will be in the future relationship between the two communities seems not to be answerable at this time.

In contrast, the relationship of the State of Israel with the American Jewish community has a measurable continuing influence on that community. The character of the influence seems to be expanding, and it does not seem to be reversible. That is so even though in the history of the American Jewish community there had been a deep cleavage over the issue of Israel from the beginnings through the 1930s.

On our account, the cleavage reflected the fundamental disagreement about the nature of emancipation, a disagreement which persists in a different form. The American Jewish community has essentially adopted the assumptions and program of the emancipation as we have outlined them, while the Zionist movement was skeptical of those assumptions and rejected the program. That is why American Zionist thinkers, like Louis Brandeis, Judah Magnes, and Mordecai M. Kaplan, developed reinterpretations of Zionism. In those reinterpretations, the long-term viability of Judaism under conditions of freedom in the United States was asserted. At the same time, American Jewish support for a national homeland in Palestine was called for because such a homeland could serve as a refuge for other communities or as a locus of Jewish cultural or religious renascence. Yet Zionism remained a controversial, even minority, position within the American Jewish community. Accordingly, as we have noted, it received the support of many groups within the community but was not part of the consensually adopted communal agenda of the community. In the 1930s, with the need of a refuge for victims of Nazi Germany, and in the 1940s, after the destruction of European Jewry, this cleavage disappeared. After the rise of the State of Israel, it is not only true that the American Jewish community became overwhelmingly pro-Israel, but involvement with Israel became a major portion of the Jewish communal agenda.

The involvement with the State of Israel has changed the Jewish community in several important ways. Here too a comparison with the ideological projection of the emancipation can sharpen the focus. In the historical perspective of the emancipation, the American Jewish community should have a tripartite identity: political, social, and religious. The political identity would be American since it would be illegitimate, with separation of church and state, to involve private religious views in political decision-making. The social identity would be a plural mix involving association in nonsectarian groups, such as academic societies, trade unions, professional groups, civic associations, and concomitantly fraternal or communal organizations. The essentially Jewish expression would be the religious affiliation, understood as a matter of private belief and rite. It was, therefore, not closely connected with ethnicity and, necessarily, distant from political attitude or political expression.

It is interesting to realize how great is the difference between this schema and the actual patterns of ethnic acculturation and religious identification of minorities in the United States. The Irish Catholic, Greek Orthodox, and Armenian Christian communities have certainly found some measure of relationship between their religious, ethnic, and political attitudes. The patterns of social association, even residential cohesiveness, in the American city have obviously been strikingly shaped by the factor of ethnicity. For the Jewish group, religion has never been understood as an affair of private belief or rite. Consequently the Jewish communal involvement with such political questions as the survival of the State of

Israel or the right of Soviet Jews to leave the Soviet Union has been continuous with religious expression.

The activities of the American Jewish community that relate to the State of Israel, in particular, have expanded greatly. These have shaped the American Jewish community in several ways. They have brought the Jewish community into a much more active political stance in order to assert its support for the survival of the State of Israel. This has led to changes in the organizational structure of the Jewish community and to the growth of a Jewish communal civil servant with different functions than those of the traditional religious, educational, or social-welfare professional leader of the community. Concomitant with this was an expansion of the fund-raising responsibilities of the community. Support for Israel motivated a significant increase in the amount of funds raised, while the allocation of funds to the needs of Israeli health, education, or welfare agencies becomes competitive with local needs.

The involvement of American Jews with Israel has not been limited to political support and financial contributions. A visit to Israel or repeated visits to Israel have increasingly become a part of the American Jewish life-style. Such visits usually include the setting up of lasting contacts with close or distant relatives who are involved in a distinctively Jewish environment. They therefore tend to greatly heighten the self-identification as Jews of American Jews. For most American Jews, the visit to Israel also often involves the first informal educational experience in the study of the roots of Jewish history. Consequently it has become a major instrument of adult self-education by the American Jewish community.

It seems plausible, consequently, to suggest that the involvement with Israel has resulted in a resurgence of ethnicity within an American Jewish community that had been characterized by a flight from ethnicity. I readily concede the speculative element in this suggestion. After all, the resurgence of ethnicity in American culture generally seems to have been heavily influenced, particularly in the youth or student culture, by the decision of the leadership of the black movement in the late 1960s to move from support of integration to identification with black nationalism. Further, as I shall indicate, there are other local factors within the American environment that generate tendencies to assert or to withdraw from ethnic identification. In many contexts, however, it is possible to show how imports of Israeli folk culture fulfill the ethnic role that the parent immigrant culture did in American Jewish cultural expression.

Even more speculatively, I suggest that involvement with Israel has also affected the moral attitudes of the American Jewish community. For historical reasons that are connected with the Jewish involvement with the emancipation, I believe, the Jews had tended to adopt a morality of ultimate universalist ideals that were closely identified with the political ideals of welfare-state liberalism or social democracy. This morality also made Jews disproportionately vulnerable to utopian movements. Support for the State of Israel, however, demands of Jews a morality of institutional responsibility which is extremely realistic in its awareness of the value claims of security, order, and other traditionally conservative values. The result is an interesting paradox. Israeli society provides American Jews with an interesting model of a "Jewish" society which has liberal social attitudes and many socialist institutions. Support of that society, however, forces upon American Jews a recognition of the nature of moral realism. This realism comprises a recognition of the need for armaments and of the legitimacy of policies in defense of the national interest. It results in an accompanying maturation of moral attitudes that is remote from utopianism. Accordingly, the involvement with Israel generates for American Jews a moral tension which, I believe, is useful for the shaping of the character of that community.

Despite this complex relationship with Israel, it is clear that the character of the Jewish community ultimately depends upon its own internal tendencies within the United States. One approach to adumbrating some of those tendencies is to delineate the nature of the American Jewish community today as a post-emancipation and post-immigrant community.

The American Jewish Community as a Post-Emancipation Community

In referring to the Jewish community as a post-emancipation community, I suggest that the United States is the one major center of Jewish population in which the program of the emancipation, as I have outlined it, has been carried out. This is so even though, ironically, the great efforts to achieve emancipation that dominated the modern history of the European Jewish communities were not undertaken in the United States. The legal and social framework of Jewish emancipation that was advocated in Europe, in the face of resistance from traditional historical institutions that had their roots in medieval Europe, was part of the constitutional structure of the United States from the birth of the country. The internal changes within the Jewish community that were advocated by the emancipation, with significant qualification in the context of the United States, became the pattern of American Jewish life as a result of the transfer of European Jewish institutions to America by successive waves of immigrants.

Throughout most of its history, the American Jewish community was involved in the adjustment of immigrant culture to the patterns of an emancipated Jewish community. At present, for the first time, a post-immigrant American Jewish generation confronts an agenda of communal continuity which can assume that the program of the emancipation has been completed. The Western European Jewish communities which might have served as a model on directions for a post-emancipation Jewish community were destroyed by Nazism. That destruction also is a formative factor in shaping the policies with which the Jewish community of the United States tries to shape its future.

From the perspective of the American Jewish community as a post-emancipation and post-immigration community, I propose to examine the directions of future Jewish communal policy and attitudes. First, I shall examine three issues that comprise what may be termed communal social policy. These issues are Jewish support for civil rights, Jewish policy on separation of church and state, and the communal Jewish response to anti-Semitism. Second, I shall consider recent developments within the religious aspects of Jewish communal life in the United States. These developments suggest a growing polarization between a more intensified religious group within the community and a much more apathetic and withdrawing group of the community. To a degree, this polarization can be related to changes in the American family pattern and to changes in Jewish demography in the recent past.

Communal Social Policy: Civil Rights

The program of the emancipation assigned a special priority to achieving full equality before the law, that is, full civil rights, for the Jewish community. Consequently, it involved the Jewish community in a principled struggle for the civil rights of all minority ethnic or religious groups, not only for the Jewish group. This involvement has remained the heritage of major Jewish groups and has led to much activity on behalf of civil rights as a major area of Jewish concern. Through the 1930s, efforts in this area were often directed to countering the racist and anti-Semitic movements in the United States, which seemed in some ways to parallel European Nazism. In the postwar period, particularly in the 1960s, the locus of these efforts often shifted to the movement in support of the civil rights of black citizens in the United States. The future direction of Jewish support of civil rights activities is currently the subject of debate within the community.

There is an unbroken consensus on the principled and pragmatic interest of the Jewish community on continuing efforts to assure every minority group in the United States of its full civil rights, both in theory and in practice. There is disagreement on some questions of policy and of priority.

The ideal which motivated Jewish action in support of civil rights from the emancipation through to the present was an ideal of equality of opportunity for all citizens, with no discrimination on grounds of race or religion. In the late 1960s, as is well known, various civil rights movements contended that this ideal was inadequate since it did not result in actual equality of results for groups which had historically been the victims of past discrimination. Accordingly, these groups argued that the goals of civil libertarians should move beyond nondiscrimination and equality of opportunity toward affirmative action in behalf of equality of result. It was conceded that such a shift would require the abandonment of the traditional attitude that mandated blindness or indifference to the race or religion of the individual. Supporters of this shift argued that the identification of the race, for example, of candidates for employment or students for admission would then permit the setting of targets for the employment or admission of members of a previously excluded minority race. The ideal of equality and of a plural society in which all groups participated, and none were excluded, would then be more fully realized.

This shift in policy involved more than the abandonment of the long dominant effort toward a kind of nondiscriminatory egalitarianism. It raised the possibility of a strategy of preferential or reverse discrimination as a legitimate method for achieving equality in American society. It raised the specter of the introduction of a quota system based on the religious or ethnic origins of individuals. It also probed the significance of the value of allocating rewards on the basis of competitively tested or ranked relevant merit for an egalitarian society.

It goes beyond our present purpose to enter into the merits of the conflicting policies or to clarify the grounds for each view. In the context of Jewish communal policy, some major Jewish organizations supported the new directions of "affirmative action," and others were concerned by the risks and inadequacies of these directions. Similar issues arose when the general consensus for nonsegregated open housing was presented with some of the dilemmas involved in potentially segregated public housing for the poor. Analogously, there is now division on the consequences of various methods for achieving the goal of an integrated school system. Some major Jewish organizations have supported busing programs as a moral imperative; others have argued that it fosters abandonment of the public school system and consequent resegregation. Since several of these dilemmas are unresolved, there is a breakdown of the consensus required for the initiation of intense effort. The Jewish community organizations that had been in the forefront of activist initiatives in the civil rights area are consequently caught in a more passive phase in the middle of the 1970s.

These dilemmas over the nature of social equality and over the strategies for attaining it coincided with a rift within the coalition that had been concerned with the extension of civil liberties from the days of the New Deal. The history of that coalition is complex, and the listing of the groups involved risks oversimplification. I shall carry out such an oversimplification solely to provide the context for the current issue in Jewish communal policy. Support for legislation against social or economic discrimination in the past was obtained from a coalition comprising the following four segments: first, the many ethnic immigrant groups that had a strong interest in the abolition of economic and social discrimination in the United States; second, the black community, which looked forward to the ending of patterns of segregation within American society; third, the Jewish community, which shared the concerns of other ethnic minorities as well as the sensitivities of a historically persecuted religious minority; fourth, members of various "liberal" constituencies, often including liberal clergy or ideological partisans. Within that coalition, there emerged important cleavages, which intensified during the late 1960s with the heightening of social tensions and ideological division on questions like urban crime, student disorder, and American foreign policy.

Within the ethnic immigrant groups, many working-class individuals believed that the liberal policies of such a coalition were adverse to their perceived economic or social interests or in conflict with their moral perceptions and attitudes. Within the black community, many groups rejected the coalition consensus, which had always advocated peaceful methods for moving toward a racially integrated society. These groups occasionally advocated violence, argued for a policy of nationalist separatism, and, in some cases, employed anti-Semitic rhetoric. Within some elements of the ideological liberal segment of the coalition, there was support for the "Palestinian" cause and criticism of the policies of the State of Israel. These trends have been disconcerting to many Jewish organizations which had been in the vanguard of the struggle for civil liberties and social equality. Consequently, there has been some reexamination of traditional Jewish communal policies although no new policy has emerged. For the future, I think it is fair to conclude that the Jewish community leadership will aim for a reconstitution of what it believes, correctly or incorrectly, to be a coalition that can help bring into being a more just society.

It should be noted that this crisis in Jewish communal policy approach took place at a time when national and international developments brought about a sense of urgency about several areas of concern. The decay of the urban center of many American cities had resulted in a significant population of Jewish elderly and poor who found themselves living under conditions of personal insecurity and environmental deprivation. The result was a demand for a Jewish communal policy which addressed itself to that neglected constituency. At the same time, at the end of the 1960s data accumulated on an apparently heightened withdrawal by Jewish youth from the Jewish community. The result, again, was a demand for a Jewish communal policy which would focus its attention on support of those institutions, like Jewish schools or counseling services, which function to enhance a sense of Jewish identity. These developments, coupled with the need for financial and political support of the State of Israel and of the emigration of Soviet Jews, lent weight to a shift in Jewish communal priorities toward a more particularistic effort at meeting the needs of the Jewish group, rather than participating in general programs of social action. The evidence for such a shift, however, is impressionistic, and there are no studies of the relevant data that provide reliable confirmation. Such a shift in communal policy might appear to be taking place because of an increase in polarization within the Jewish community. On that interpretation, the views of the pole of the Jewish community that advocates that the community move forward boldly into the new agenda of civil rights and social action have diminished in number but increased in intensity. Similarly, the pole of the Jewish community that advocates a withdrawal from the social action agenda and a reordering of priorities in terms of internal Jewish concerns has also become more articulate and intense. The resolution of the polarization, if this interpretation is correct, will determine several directions of Jewish communal policy in the future.

Communal Social Policy: Church and State

There have also been changes in attitude in an area of communal policy where there has long been consensus: separation of church and state. As we have pointed out, such separation was part of the fundamental program of Jewish emancipation in making possible a neutral area of public activity in which people of diverse religious backgrounds could participate. To be sure, there have been some areas—the chaplaincy is the most notable illustration—where an alternative model of voluntary religious pluralism supported by government has been recognized. The public school, however, has long seemed to be paradigmatic of the neutral common ground where the private religious backgrounds of students or teachers should not penetrate.

There has been some element of change in this attitude. Some groups have called for the legitimacy of ethnic heritage studies in the public school or of other programs that replace neutrality with pluralism. There has also been a degree of disaffection with the public schools as evidenced by the continuation of a private school system in a period of inflationary school costs. Within the Jewish milieu, however, the significant factor has been the initiative of the extreme Orthodox community that immigrated to America after the Second World War in setting up a Jewish parochial school network. Like other parochial school systems, the Orthodox Jewish system seeks to develop constitutionally appropriate mechanisms for publicly funded support of parochial schools. There has been continuous opposition to public funding of parochial or private education by major Jewish communal groups. This opposition has been motivated by the commitment within the Jewish community to the separation of church and state. Critics of this opposition have charged that it has the effect of denying possible economic support for the education of the children of the most religiously devout and least affluent members of the community. Despite the basis this disagreement provides for polarization, it is unlikely that it will develop. First, there has been an increasing trend within Jewish communal organizations to support Jewish education, including Jewish parochial schools. Second, the decisions to be made by the courts on constitutional grounds provide the basis for consensus regardless of the particular preferences or interests of various segments of the community.

Communal Social Policy: Anti-Semitism

There have been significant changes in the public position of the Jewish community within American society since the Second World War. Before the war, the main areas of Jewish residence were the ethnic neighborhoods of the major cities, particularly in the Northeast. Since the war, Jews have migrated to the suburbs as well as to the South and to the western parts of the United States. Concomitantly, there have been changes in the Jewish occupational and employment structure that reflect the entry of Jews into universities, professions, and corporations where there had previously been restricted access. This erosion of discrimination against Jews, both in patterns of residence and employment, and even, to a degree, in social discrimination, has not eliminated Jewish concern about anti-Semitic prejudice and practice. It is universally recognized that the general democratic ethos within American society, the social mobility of the American economy, and the strength of the nondiscriminatory character of the American legal institutions have been crucial in the progress of the Jewish community in the United States. At the same time, a continuing area of communal concern within the Jewish community is the effort to eradicate anti-Semitic prejudice and to combat the practices that may reflect or institutionalize such prejudice. What may uniquely characterize the present circumstance is the presence of contrary assessments of the strength of contemporary American anti-Semitism and of conflicting prognoses of the future.

On one account, the relevant factor is the decline of what is termed "nativist" anti-Semitism, which presumably was prevalent among populist groups like the Ku Klux Klan and similar racist movements in the 1920s and 1930s. This decline has been accompanied by the moratorium on public expressions of anti-Semitism which has prevailed in American society since the Second World War. Since the war, a pattern of legal and institutional safeguards against discrimination has developed. Finally, the widespread expectation that Jews would become the scapegoat for the oil embargo imposed during the Middle Eastern war was not realized. Accordingly, though all social tendencies are theoretically reversible, the optimistic assessment finds little basis in the present trends of American society for a revival of anti-Semitism.

The pessimistic assessment cites the legitimization of anti-Semitism through the political attack on Zionism. Anti-Zionism as a device for attacking the State of Israel has received a measure of support from governmental opponents of Israel, including the Soviet Union and many Arab countries. Such an attack inevitably involves the propagandistic use of anti-Jewish stereotypes and canards. Sympathizers with the political policies of the Soviet Union or the Arab countries, usually because of their support for the interests of the "Palestinians," provide a base for the dissemination of anti-Semitic propaganda. There is, on the pessimistic view, an enduring historical basis for anti-Jewish prejudice 'in all Western societies. Currently, there is also an inevitable fading of the memories of the Nazi experience which had served to inhibit the expression of such prejudice. Accordingly, given a legitimization for anti-Semitic prejudice and a powerful interest in its dissemination, there is a rational expectation that a new wave of anti-Semitic sentiment will eventuate.

It is beyond our scope and competence to judge between these conflicting assessments. The range of opinion indicates the complexity of the task confronting those Jewish agencies which are committed to programs for the elimination of anti-Semitic prejudice. Though the priorities of the Jewish communal agenda are shifting, as we shall indicate below, the concern over the potential eruption of anti-Semitic prejudice effectively guarantees the continuity of Jewish communal efforts in interreligious and intergroup relations.

Changes in the Religious Attitudes of the American Jewish Community

Judaism has always comprised both an aspect of religion and an aspect of peoplehood. Accordingly, change in communal social policy, as it affects the ethnic or peoplehood character of Jewish existence, cannot be examined independently of some consideration of the changing character of religious belief and attitudes. In the recent past, there have been several noteworthy developments.

The historical background for recent development is the framework which grew up after the emancipation. As we have seen,

Orthodox Judaism was confronted by the demand for adjustment to the new social and intellectual currents of Europe in the nineteenth century. The result was the growth of the secular Jewish ideologies we have mentioned and also the development of new religious trends—Neo-Orthodoxy, Conservatism, and Reform. American Judaism, as a post-emancipation community, has been structured by these three trends. Each trend has developed a network of associated synagogues, a major rabbinical school, a recognized book of prayer, a congregational school system, and a minor galaxy of complementing institutions and organizations.

This development received its greatest impetus in the immediate postwar period. At that time, Jews in significant numbers left the urban ethnic environment in which Jewish identity had been rooted in patterns of association. They moved to suburban environments, where Jewish identity was confirmed, in the absence of the "natural" ethnic milieu, by affiliation with the local congregation. The social trends of the 1950s, with the public stress on the norm of religious identification in America, clearly provided support for this development.

Throughout this period, as had been the case since the emancipation, the burden of adjustment was on religious belief and institutions, which were required to accommodate to the patterns of the secular society. In the nineteenth century, Jewish religious leaders had sought to show that Judaism was compatible with Kantian liberalism or Hegelian historicism. In twentieth-century America, they also sought to show how it was compatible, or could be reconstructed to be compatible, with Deweyan progressivism or with liberal social philosophy or liberal religions. It was generally believed by Neo-Orthodox, Conservative, and Reform thinkers that a Judaism which failed to adjust to the temper of the times would be unable to sustain loyalty from the subsequent generation and could not survive.

In the past decade, there has been an apparent rejection of that assumption. The evidence for this rejection is twofold. It consists, first, in the evidence of growth and stability among the more extreme Orthodox groups, particularly Hassidic groups, through the entire postwar period. These groups have actively proselytized among the youth culture without accommodating their point of view to more liberal, rational, or secular patterns. Second, the usual model of generational adaptation within the United States had been one in which children of Orthodox parents tended to affiliation with Conservative or Reform movements and children of Conservative parents moved toward Reform or secular affiliation. There is evidence that this trend no longer obtains. Accordingly, the pragmatic argument for reinterpretation as a mechanism of generational adjustment has been questioned.

There exist two fairly well developed hypotheses to explain this resurgence of more Orthodox religious trends after a period of several generations of shift away from Orthodoxy within American Jewry. One hypothesis relates this change to the reevaluation of rationality in contemporary society. The second hypothesis finds the key to the change in the reevaluation of ethnicity in American society. Let us consider each hypothesis in turn for the light it may shed upon religious change in the American Jewish community.

The first hypothesis argues that traditional religion had been placed on the defensive in Western society since the Enlightenment. The ability of religion to provide men with an account of man's place in the scheme of things had been overwhelmed by the achievement of modern science, which showed itself more capable of doing this, both from the vantage point of credibility and the vantage point of utility. Even more, the tradition role of religion in providing men with moral guidance had been undermined by secular rationalism, particularly in its own faith variants like Marxist or liberal rationalist ideology.

One traditional function of religion, in which it gave people some sense of the possibilities of their own fulfillment, had been challenged or replaced by new methods or approaches in individual self-fulfillment, often linked to psychology. Until recently, the religious response to such challenges, particularly within Judaism as in liberal religion, had been to reinterpret the doctrines of traditional religion in ways which were compatible with the scientific, rational, or secular features of modernity.

According to the hypothesis under review, it is claimed that there has been a disillusion with the fruits of modernity in contemporary

Western society. There has been a revolt against the rationalist temperament and the scientific attitude toward both the nature of the world and the nature of value. The consequence of that disillusion has been the resurgence of religious belief. Presumably this hypothesis would explain the revival of extreme Orthodoxy among some segments of Jewish youth after a long period in which the dominant trend had been liberalization or erosion of Orthodox Jewish practice.

The second hypothesis advanced to explain the apparent fact of religious revival has related this revival to a new emphasis on the significance of ethnicity. On this view, the tendency within Jewish religious life to move from the separatist Orthodoxy of the Old World to the Neo-Orthodox, Conservative, and Reform Judaism of America has been an effort to transcend ethnicity. It can be understood, as can the assimilative tendencies of American Jewry in many areas of experience, from choice of name to innovations in life-style, as an effort to overcome the trauma of ghettoization. There has been, in the recent past, a reversal of the trend for transcendence of ethnicity in the Jewish community. There may be several reasons for this reversal.

One of these reasons may be the working of Hansen's law so that the post-immigrant generation is seeking to remember the ethnic culture which the immigrant generation sought to forget. A second reason may be that the "trauma of Auschwitz," with the accompanying recognition of the inadequacies of Western universalist humanitarianism in its response to the particular persecution of the Jews, serves to counter the tendency to withdraw from the ethnic community. Certainly, the association of American Jews with the struggle of Soviet Jewry, and more important, the identification of American Jews with the struggle of Israel, reinforces those ethnic patterns of association. Third, the alleged failure of the great secular faiths of the recent past, such as the Marxist faith and the rationalist confidence in the new humanist attitudes that would be generated by the scientific revolution, has led to a new search for a sense of community in smaller and more traditional cultural groups.

The search for the small, face-to-face community within the mass society has been a distinctive aspect of contemporary youth culture.

Accordingly, in the elaboration of the resurgence-of-ethnicity hypothesis, Jewish persons in America are more likely to relate to tightly knit communities which provide a strong sense of social cohesiveness. On this view, the traditionalist Orthodox synagogue provides a more authentic and cohesive sense of community than those institutions of Judaism that have been transformed by modernity.

The evidence for both of these hypotheses is similar. Both appeal to the following impressionistic data which observers of the Jewish community have noted. There has been a pronounced shift within Reform Judaism to a greater emphasis upon traditional observances. Thus, the newly adopted prayer book has restored a great measure of use of the Hebrew language in the prayers. Again, the repertoire of folk songs within Jewish youth culture is drawn from Orthodox Hassidic music or from Israeli group life. The trend to superbly designed large synagogues or temples has been replaced by a stress upon small-group activity within the synagogue. So, although the evidence is impressionistic, there is some reason to believe that there has been a significant point of inflection in the direction of religious trends within the American Jewish community.

The preceding investigation of the phenomenon of the intensification of religious practice among one segment of the American Jewish community would be incomplete and misleading if it did not include some reference to the contrary phenomenon. There is a strong assimilative tendency within the American Jewish community. There seems to be evidence that residual loyalties and traditions that functioned within the immigrant community or the children of immigrants are eroding in the present generation of American Jews. Some observers trace this to the continuing lessening of religious commitment and practice which has been a cumulative consequence of modernity. Others believe that, relatively independent of the fate of religion in America, there is an ongoing erosion of sense of Jewish identity within the Jewish community as a concomitant of the pluralism and the openness of American society.

Accordingly, the portrait which emerges is of an American Jewish community that is more polarized than it has ever been. It now comprises a more assertively Orthodox community and a more involved Zionist community than at any time in its history. At the same time, it comprises a greater segment of Jews who are indifferent to the communal feature and tend to withdraw from the community than at any previous time. In such a portrait, the determining factor may well be how the "center" groups within the community respond to these two polar tendencies. There are competing prognoses on this response.

On the one hand, those who have examined the macroscopic, demographic, and sociological data tend to project continuing erosion within the Jewish community. There are two primary factors to which reference is usually made. One is the changes within the American family, which is changing the standard ways in which Jewish families and their younger children have affiliated with the congregations and schools of the Jewish neighborhoods throughout the country. It remains to be seen whether new patterns of family relationship will sustain the patterns of Jewish affiliation that have been the conventional and traditional building blocks of the Jewish communal structure and have formed the framework for expression of Jewish personal identity.

The second factor is the leap in the intermarriage rate. The statistical data indicating a great increase in Jewish intermarriage have been confirmed in several recent studies. It has been argued that this is a natural consequence of the demographic shift of Jews from the Northeast to the South and West of the country, where the Jews form a smaller proportion of the population. This increase has also been related to the rise in the number of Jewish persons of college age who attend college. On this account, the university environment is one which is conducive to a transcendence of ethnic or religious particularism. While few data exist on the degree to which intermarriage results in the conversion of the non-Jewish partner, projections of the present rate of intermarriage and of the very low Jewish birth rate suggest a decrease of the Jewish community. This would probably have a negative impact on the effort the community has demonstrated on behalf of its cultural and religious continuity.

On the other hand, even though the demographic projections tend to be negative, those who have examined the recent history of communal policy have found grounds for optimism. Within the organized Jewish community, there has been a significant shift in direction and priorities. Without withdrawing from historically important fields of endeavor that range from services to new immigrants, defense of civil rights, and social welfare of the elderly or needy to major institutions of health care, family service, or recreation, there has been a new assertion of communal responsibility for Jewish education. A single dramatic statistical indication of this is the growth of university programs of Jewish studies. A generation ago, there were only a handful of such programs, which today number about 330. Many of these programs comprise large-scale teaching programs, significant research activity, and expanding library resources. Much more generally, however, a commitment to excellent Jewish educational institutions—day schools, camps, informal educational environments—has emerged as a priority in many local communities throughout the country.

The simultaneous existence of tendencies toward the erosion of Jewish identity and toward its strengthening has been a constant throughout Jewish history. Even further, it is a familiar historical recurrence that the so-called hard data, such as demographic trends or institutional facts of family formation, support the projection of erosion or assimilation, while the evidence for a strengthening of the Jewish community derives from "soft" data, such as changes in communal policy or records of individual decisions. Most social scientists would argue, I think, that the realities of demographic trends and seemingly irreversible institutional trends are more likely to provide an indication of the future of the community. I suppose it could be suggested that Jewish history provides the basis for an inductive argument of the significance of communal policy and individual acts of choice in preserving Jewish continuity.

On either view, however, the American Jewish community is confronted with severe challenges to its survival and to the character of its future communal culture. The understanding of these challenges and the fashioning of appropriate response is an agenda for action for those members of the historical community who share a concern for its future.

SELECTED BIBLIOGRAPHY

Elazar, Daniel. *Community and Polity: The Organizational Dynamics of American Jewry.* Philadelphia: Jewish Publication Society, 1976.

Janowsky, Oscar, ed. *The American Jew: A Reappraisal.* Philadelphia: Jewish Publication Society, 1964.

Sidorsky, David, ed. *The Future of the Jewish Community in America.* New York: Basic Books, 1973.

Sklare, Marshall, ed. *The Jew in American Society.* New York: Behrman House, 1974.

Contributors

DANIEL J. ELAZAR is Professor of Political Studies, and Head of the Institute of Local Government, at Bar-Ilan University, Israel, and Professor of Political Science, and Director of the Center for the Study of Federalism, at Temple University.

ABRAHAM J. KARP is Professor of History and Religious Studies at the University of Rochester; Visiting Professor of Jewish History at the Jewish Theological Seminary; and a member of the Institute of Contemporary Jewry, Hebrew University, Israel.

DAVID MIRSKY is Professor of English Literature at Yeshiva University; Dean of Stern College, Yeshiva University; and Vice President of Academic Affairs, Yeshiva University.

MANHEIM SHAPIRO, sociologist, educator, and social worker, is a former Executive Director of the Bureau for Careers in Jewish Service; Director of Jewish Communal Affairs for the American Jewish Committee; and National Director of Programs and Publications for the B'nai B'rith Youth Organization.

DAVID SIDORSKY is Professor of Philosophy at Columbia University; consultant to the American Jewish Committee Task Force on the Future of the Jewish Community in America; and Chairman of the Board of Trustees of the American Zionist Youth Foundation.

STANLEY M. WAGNER is Professor of Judaic Studies at the University of Denver; Director of the Center for Judaic Studies, University of

Denver; and rabbi of Beth HaMedrosh Hagadol Congregation, Denver, Colorado.

TRUDE WEISS-ROSMARIN is editor of the *Jewish Spectator;* and author of *Judaism and Christianity: The Differences; Jewish Survival; The Hebrew Moses: An Answer to Sigmund Freud;* and *Jewish Expressions on Jesus.*

Index

Aaron, 17
Abraham, 17
Acculturation. *See* Assimilation
Affirmative action, 144
Agrarianism, 107
Ahab, 18
Ahad Ha'am, 135
Americanization. *See* Assimilation
American Jewish Congress, 112
American Jewish literature, 12–13,
    79–104
  humor, 99–100
  style, 93
  themes, 85–102
  author's acceptance of Jewishness,
    100–102
  religious impulse of, 94–96
American Joint Distribution Committee,
    41
American law and Jewish participation,
    112
American political ideas
  contradiction with Jewish political
    ideas, 115–116
American political tradition, 107
Amos, 17
Angoff, Charles, 91
Anti-Semitism, 135–136, 148–149
Art and religion, 10
Arts and the Jewish tradition, 9–11,
    13–14
Assimilation, 3, 32–33, 38–39, 44–46,
    69–75, 89–90, 113, 118, 122, 141,
    153
Association of the American Hebrew
    Congregations, 61–62

Babylonian period, 4, 8

Bellow, Saul, 93–94
  Herzog, 98
  Mr. Sammler's Planet, 98
Benjamin, I. J., 54–55
Berith Kodesh Congregation, 67
Bible and political ideas, 108
B'nai B'rith, 35
Book of Life, 10–11
Brandeis, Louis, 138
Breasted, James H., 15–16
Buber, Martin, 14

Cahan, Abraham, *Rise of David Levinsky*,
    12, 85–87, 96–97
Cemeteries, 33–64
Charity, 17, 33–34, 36, 42
  Biblical and Talmudic tradition, 35
Church and state, 113–114, 146–147
  public schools, 147
Civil Rights,
  support by Jews, 143–146
Cleveland Conference, 56
Cohen, Hermann, 14
Compassion, 11
Conference on Jewish Cultural Arts, 13
Congregations, 26–34, 70–71
  list of prepared in 1854, 65–66
Conservative Judaism, 40, 60–63,
    133–134
Creative arts, 81

Damascus massacre, 55
David, King, 16
de Tocqueville, Alexis, 53
Democratic Party and the American Jew,
    117–118
Discrimination, 27, 35, 43, 113, 148–149
Doctorow, D. L., 94